FIGHTING
FASCISM

FIGHTING FASCISM

HOW TO STRUGGLE
AND HOW TO WIN

CLARA ZETKIN

Edited and introduced by Mike Taber and John Riddell

Haymarket Books
Chicago, Illinois

© 2017 Mike Taber and John Riddell

Published in 2017 by
Haymarket Books
P.O. Box 180165
Chicago, IL 60618
773-583-7884
www.haymarketbooks.org
info@haymarketbooks.org

ISBN: 978-1-60846-852-2

Trade distribution:
In the US, Consortium Book Sales and Distribution, www.cbsd.com
In Canada, Publishers Group Canada, www.pgcbooks.ca
In the UK, Turnaround Publisher Services, www.turnaround-uk.com
All other countries, Ingram Publisher Services International,
IPS_Intlsales@ingramcontent.com

This book was published with the generous support of Lannan Foundation and Wallace Action Fund.

Cover design by Josh On.

Printed in Canada by union labor.

Library of Congress Cataloging-in-Publication data is available.

10 9 8 7 6 5 4 3 2

CONTENTS

INTRODUCTION

Seldom has there been a word more bandied about, yet less understood, than *fascism*.

For many, the fascist label is simply an insult, directed against particularly repellent and reactionary individuals or movements. It's also customarily used as a political description of right-wing military dictatorships.

The term took on new significance during the 2016 US presidential election, in which the ultimate victor Donald Trump was routinely compared to Benito Mussolini and other fascist leaders. "Fascist comparisons are not new in American politics," stated an article in the May 28, 2016, *New York Times*. "But with Mr. Trump, such comparisons have gone beyond the fringe and entered mainstream conversation both in the United States and abroad."

Although these particular comparisons are overdrawn and imprecise, all allegations of fascism must be examined seriously. Working people and the oppressed have every reason to fear the endemic racism, abolition of labor and civil rights, brutal repression, and mass murder that characterize fascism.

While resemblances on some level can undoubtedly be found among most rightist movements and regimes, fascism itself is a very specific phenomenon, with unique features. Understanding the characteristics and dynamics of fascism is not just an academic exercise. Doing so is essential for being able to combat it.

This short book, containing a report and resolution by Clara Zetkin at a 1923 leadership meeting of the Communist International, presents a far-reaching analysis of what was then something entirely new on the world scene.

Many readers will be struck by the clarity and foresight of Zetkin's assessment, delivered at a time when fascism's emergence was still a mystery to most observers. Reviewing it almost a century later, one can appreciate her accomplishment in outlining, at this early date, a consistent Marxist position on the nature of fascism and how to fight it.

Fascism's emergence

The origins of fascism can be found in post–World War I Italy. Organized by Benito Mussolini during a period of social crisis in 1919, the Fasci Italiani di Combattimento arose as a reaction to the rising movement of the proletariat, that is, the social class of those who depend on sale of their labor power for their means of subsistence.

During this time Italian workers, inspired by the victory of the Russian Revolution and battered by Italian capitalism's postwar crisis, were marching forward in militant struggle. Throughout all layers of Italian society, expectation was high that the Italian Socialist Party—then a member of the Communist International—was on the verge of coming to power.

The proletarian upsurge reached a high point in September 1920. During that month over half a million workers, led by the metalworkers, seized factories throughout Italy. Workers began to organize production under the leadership of factory councils, and in many places they formed Red Guards to defend the seized factories. The strikes spread to the railways and other workplaces, and many poor peasants and agricultural workers carried out land seizures. Effective appeals were made to soldiers, as fellow workers in uniform, to refuse to obey any orders to attack the factories. In face of this seemingly unstoppable wave, the capitalist class and its government were paralyzed with indecision and fear. A revolutionary situation was unfolding, with the conquest of political power on the agenda.

But the Italian Socialist Party and the main trade union federation under its influence refused to see this month-long revolutionary movement as anything more than a simple union struggle. With such a mindset, the union leadership eventually directed the workers to leave the factories in exchange for a package of enticing but empty promises by the capitalists—who by that time were willing to sign anything provided they could get their factories back. Italian working people, who had hoped and expected that the end of capitalist rule was near, abandoned the factories in dejection.

The failure of the factory occupation movement led to widespread demoralization within the working class. The Fasci stepped up recruitment and carried out an escalating wave of attacks against the labor movement, receiving growing financial support from leading capitalists and protection from police and other sectors of the Italian state. In 1921 and 1922 several thousand workers and peasants were murdered in fascist "punitive expeditions." Hundreds of labor halls and union headquarters were destroyed.

Rapidly assuming the character of a mass movement, the fascists were able to take control of the government at the end of October 1922, with Mussolini becoming prime minister. Once in power, fascism proceeded to crush the unions entirely, along with all other independent workers' organizations.

Encouraged by the Italian fascist victory, similar movements arose in other European countries, the strongest being in Germany. Fascist-type formations were also seen in Poland, Czechoslovakia, Austria, and elsewhere.

Recognizing a new phenomenon

As with most new social phenomena, it was not immediately apparent what was involved. Initially, many tended to lump fascism together with other instances of counterrevolutionary violence and terror.

In the years after the First World War, such terror was indeed widespread. In Hungary, a defeated revolution that briefly held power in 1919 was followed by 5,000 executions and 75,000 jailings. In Finland, where a civil war had taken place, the toll was 10,000 shot and 100,000 sent to concentration camps.

Comparable instances of what became known as "white terror" were seen in other countries.

While the Italian fascists' use of counterrevolutionary violence was certainly analogous, the phenomenon of fascism involved something more. Uncovering its true nature was a task that fell to the Communist International.

Founded in 1919 under the impact of the Russian Revolution, the Communist International (Comintern) was something entirely new: a movement dedicated to discussing how the working class could overthrow capitalist rule, and organizing to do so. Under Lenin, the Comintern's congresses and meetings were schools of revolutionary politics.

The Comintern had its first organized discussion of fascism at its Fourth Congress in November 1922. It was not particularly fruitful, however. A report by Italian Communist Amadeo Bordiga, while describing important aspects of Mussolini's movement in Italy, was less successful in uncovering fascism's nature, stressing instead the similarities between fascism and bourgeois democracy and predicting that Italian fascism would not last long. Neither Bordiga's report nor the discussion that followed paid much attention to the struggle against fascism.[1]

Realizing they hadn't yet gotten to the bottom of things, in June 1923 the Comintern's leaders took up the question once again. The venue was the Third Enlarged Plenum of the Communist International's Executive Committee. The key person in this effort was Clara Zetkin, who gave the report to that meeting and authored the resolution it adopted.

Clara Zetkin

Sixty-six years old in 1923, Clara Zetkin was one of the Comintern's most prominent veteran fighters. She was a unique figure in the international revolutionary movement.

In 1878, at the age of 21, Zetkin joined the socialist movement in Germany. That was the year in which the Anti-Socialist Laws were enacted in Germany, making public advocacy of socialism a crime and membership in the Social Democratic Party (SPD) illegal. But Zetkin refused to be intimidated. Forced into exile for several years, she increased her activity in the revolutionary movement and became a leading activist in the party. In 1891 she began to edit *Die Gleichheit,* the SPD's newspaper directed at women.

In 1907 Zetkin was the central founding leader of the international socialist women's movement. One of the most important initiatives of that movement was the establishment of March 8 as International Women's Day, a decision made at its 1910 conference.

A collaborator of Rosa Luxemburg, Zetkin belonged to the left wing of the SPD. In 1914, when that party betrayed its socialist principles by openly supporting Germany's war effort in World War I, Zetkin broke with the party's declaration of a "civil peace" with German capitalism for the war's duration, and went into active opposition. Becoming part of the revolutionary underground organized in the Spartacus League, she was arrested several times for antiwar activities. In 1918 the Spartacus League helped found the Communist Party (CP), of which Zetkin became a leader.

Following the murder of Luxemburg, Karl Liebknecht, and others in early 1919, Zetkin came to play a central role within the Communist Party leadership, as she did within the Communist International as a whole.

While Zetkin is best known for her decades-long role as the central figure in the socialist and communist women's movement, she was much more. She was a well-rounded political leader capable of deep political analysis and drawing practical conclusions from it, as was demonstrated by her 1923 report on fascism.

Fascism's characteristics

In that report, Zetkin pointed to some of the key features of fascism:

- Fascism's emergence is inextricably tied to the economic crisis of capitalism and the decline of its institutions. This crisis is characterized by escalating attacks on the working class, and by middle layers of society being increasingly squeezed and driven down into the proletariat.

  "Fascism is rooted, indeed, in the dissolution of the capitalist economy and the bourgeois state. . . . The war shattered the capitalist economy down to its foundations. This is evident not only in the appalling impoverishment of the proletariat, but also in the proletarianization of very broad petty-bourgeois and middle-bourgeois masses."

- The rise of fascism is based on the proletariat's failure to resolve capitalism's social crisis by taking power and beginning to reorganize society. This failure of working-class leadership breeds demoralization among workers and among the forces within society that had looked to the proletariat and socialism as a way out of the crisis.

  These social forces, Zetkin indicated, had hoped that "socialism could bring about global change. These expectations were painfully shattered. . . . [T]hey lost their belief not only in the reformist leaders but also in socialism itself."

- Fascism possesses a mass character, with a special appeal to petty-bourgeois layers threatened by the decline of the capitalist order.

  The capitalist decline results in "the proletarianization of very broad petty-bourgeois and middle-bourgeois masses, the calamitous conditions among small peasants, and the bleak distress of the 'intelligentsia'. . . . What weighs on them above all is the lack of security for their basic existence."

- To win support from these layers, fascism makes use of anticapitalist demagogy.

  "Masses in their thousands streamed to fascism. It became an asylum for all the politically homeless, the socially uprooted, the destitute and disillusioned. . . . The petty-bourgeois and intermediate social forces at first vacillate indecisively between the powerful historical camps of the proletariat and bourgeoisie. They are induced to sympathize with the proletariat by their life's suffering and, in part, by their soul's noble longings and high ideals, so long as it is revolutionary in its conduct and seems to have prospects for victory. Under the pressure of the masses and their needs, and influenced by this situation, even the fascist leaders are forced to at least flirt with the revolutionary proletariat, even though they may not have any sympathy with it."

- Fascist ideology elevates nation and state above all class contradictions and class interests.

   "[W]hat [the masses] no longer hoped for from the revolutionary proletarian class and from socialism, they now hoped would be achieved by the most able, strong, determined, and bold elements of every social class. All these forces must come together in a community. And this community, for the fascists, is the nation. . . . The instrument to achieve fascist ideals is, for them, the state. A strong and authoritarian state that will be their very own creation and their obedient tool. This state will tower high above all differences of party and class."

- The ideology of national chauvinism is used by fascist leaders as a cover to incite militarism and imperialist war.

   "The armed forces [of fascist Italy] were to serve only to defend the fatherland. That was the promise. But the burgeoning size of the army and the enormous scope of armaments are oriented to major imperialist adventures. . . . Hundreds of millions of lire have been approved for heavy industry to build the most modern machines and murderous instruments of death."

• A major characteristic of fascism is the use of organized violence by anti-working-class shock troops, aiming to crush all independent proletarian activity.

In Italy, Mussolini's forces engaged in "direct, bloody terror," Zetkin pointed out. Starting in agricultural areas, the fascists "struck out against the rural proletarians, whose organizations were devastated and burned out and whose leaders were murdered." Later "the fascist terror extend[ed] to the proletarians of the large cities."

• The ideology of racism and racist scapegoating is central to fascism's message. While this aspect was not yet entirely clear in 1923, Zetkin nevertheless pointed out how in Germany "the fascist program is exhausted by the phrase, 'Beat up the Jews.'"

• At a certain point, important sections of the capitalist class begin to support and finance the fascist movement, seeing it as a way to counter the threat of proletarian revolution.

"The bourgeoisie can no longer rely on its state's regular means of force to secure its class rule. For that it needs an extralegal and nonstate instrument of force. That has been offered by the motley assemblage that makes up the fascist mob." The capitalists "openly sponsored fascist terrorism, supporting it with money and in other ways."

- Once in power, fascism tends to become bureaucratized, and moves away from its earlier demagogic appeals, leading to a resurgence of class contradictions and class struggle.

"There is a blatant contradiction between what fascism promised and what it delivered to the masses. All the talk about how the fascist state will place the interests of the nation above everything, once exposed to the wind of reality, burst like a soap bubble. The 'nation' revealed itself to be the bourgeoisie; the ideal fascist state revealed itself to be the vulgar, unscrupulous bourgeois class state. . . . Class contradictions are mightier than all the ideologies that deny their existence."

Alternate analyses

Zetkin's analysis of fascism was radically different from other ones then being put forward within the workers' and socialist movements.

Among these, Zetkin's report took up the view of the reformist Social Democrats. "For them fascism is nothing but terror and violence," she reported.

"The reformists view fascism as an expression of the unshakable and all-conquering power and strength of bourgeois class rule. The proletariat is not up to the task of taking up the struggle against it—that would be presumptuous and doomed to failure. So there is nothing left for the proletariat but to step aside quietly and modestly, and not provoke the tigers and lions of bourgeois class rule through a struggle for its liberation and its own rule."

Zetkin's analysis also contrasts sharply with the analysis of fascism put forward subsequently by the Stalin-led Communist parties in the years and decades ahead. There were two main Stalinist approaches, both of which are counterposed to Zetkin's perspective:

1. *Social fascism.* Adopted during the Comintern's ultraleft 'Third Period' of the late 1920s and early 1930s, the thrust of this view was to equate Social Democracy and fascism, thereby justifying the German Communist Party's refusal to seek a united front with the powerful Social Democratic Party in the fight against the Nazis.

    Had such a united front been organized, it would have had the support of the overwhelming majority of working people in Germany and would almost certainly have been powerful enough to counter the Nazis. The adamant refusal to do so by both the CP and SPD leaderships can rightly be said to have opened the door to Hitler's assumption of power.

2. *Popular frontism.* This view was first fully presented in a report by Georgi Dimitrov to the Seventh Congress of the by-then fully Stalinized Comintern in 1935. Fascism, Dimitrov stated, was "the open terrorist dictatorship of the most reactionary, most chauvinistic and most imperialist elements of finance capital." It "acts in the interests

of the extreme imperialists," which he characterized as "the most reactionary circles of the bourgeoisie."[2]

Based on this analysis, the central task was to form blocs—"popular fronts"—with supposedly less reactionary, less chauvinistic, and less imperialist elements of the bourgeoisie—its "antifascist wing"—and to subordinate independent working-class struggle and political action to this objective. In practice such an approach meant that Stalinist parties stood in opposition to independent proletarian revolutionary action in general, seeing this as an obstacle to the projected popular front. Such a perspective also became justification for giving back-handed support to "antifascist" capitalist politicians such as Franklin D. Roosevelt in the United States, on the pretext that his Republican opponent represented "the chief menace of fascism."[3]

Leon Trotsky took the lead in rejecting these Stalinist positions, defending the key points raised by Zetkin in 1923. Written in polemical form, Trotsky's writings during the 1930s on the rise of fascism in Germany and the lessons of the Nazi victory present some of the clearest expositions of the Marxist analysis of fascism and what is required to defeat it.[4]

How to fight fascism

Liberal procapitalist forces frequently suggest that if fascist figures are just ignored, they will go away. That was not the view of

Zetkin, however. For her, there was a life-and-death need for the working class and its allies to mobilize their full power in opposition to fascism.

In discussing the working-class fight against fascism, Zetkin emphasized several points:

- Workers' self-defense is crucial in order to confront the fascist terror campaign. Above all, this includes organized workers' defense guards to combat fascist attacks.

  "At present the proletariat has urgent need for self-defense against fascism, and this self-protection against fascist terror must not be neglected for a single moment. At stake is the proletarians' personal safety and very existence, as well as the survival of their organizations. Self-defense of proletarians is the need of the hour. We must not combat fascism in the way of the reformists in Italy, who beseeched them to 'leave me alone, and then I'll leave you alone.' On the contrary! Meet violence with violence. But not violence in the form of individual terror—that will surely fail. But rather violence as the power of the revolutionary organized proletarian class struggle."

- United-front action to combat fascism is essential, involving all working-class organizations and currents, regardless of political differences.

  "[P]roletarian struggle and self-defense against fascism requires the proletarian united front. Fascism does not ask if the worker in the factory has a soul painted in the white and blue colors of Bavaria; the black, red, and gold colors of the bourgeois republic; or the red banner with the hammer and sickle. It does not ask whether the worker wants to restore the Wittelsbach dynasty [of Bavaria], is an enthusiastic fan of [SPD leader and German President Friedrich] Ebert, or would prefer to see our friend [CP leader Heinrich] Brandler as president of the German Soviet Republic. All that matters to fascism is that they encounter a class-conscious proletarian, and then they club him to the ground. That is why workers must come together for struggle without distinctions of party or trade-union affiliation."

- In addition to combating fascism physically when necessary to defend itself, the working class needs to combat fascism's mass appeal politically, making special efforts among middle-class layers.

  "[T]he [Italian Communist] party surely also made a policy error in viewing fascism solely as a military phenomenon and overlooking its ideological and political side. Let us not forget that before beating down the proletariat through acts of terror, fascism in Italy had already won an ideological and political victory over the workers' movement that lay at the root of its triumph. It would be very dangerous to fail to consider the importance of overcoming fascism ideologically and politically."

- Combating fascism in this way means, above all, demonstrating the proletarian leadership's absolute determination to fight to take power out of the hands of the bourgeoisie in order to resolve capitalism's social crisis, and putting forward a program aimed at cementing the alliances necessary to do so.

Zetkin believed that the perspective of a revolutionary fight for governmental power, based on an alliance of the exploited and oppressed social classes, was essential for victory over fascism. For this reason, in her report she stressed that a governmental demand expressing this perspective—that of a workers' and peasants' government—"is virtually a requirement for the struggle to defeat fascism."

The threat of fascism today

Striving to understand fascism today is not merely a historical question.

As the twenty-first century unfolds, capitalism has entered a period of social crisis, marked by escalating attacks on the rights and living conditions of working people and all the oppressed, along with sharpening social polarization. The November 2016 election of billionaire capitalist Donald Trump as US president, following a campaign marked by brazen rightist demagogy and openly racist appeals, was both a reflection and a sharpening of this crisis.

As Zetkin foresaw almost a century ago, it is precisely situations like this that can give rise to fascist movements at a certain stage.

Such movements recognize the social crisis, but they aim to shift the blame for it away from the capitalist system, looking instead for scapegoats: immigrants, Blacks, Jews, self-confident and independent women, LGBT people, Roma people, and others. Outlandish conspiracy theories are conjured up, designed to deflect attention away from the social and economic system responsible for the crisis.

To garner support, fascist movements play on resentment. They appeal to racist, chauvinist, and antiwoman sentiments that deeply pervade so-called popular culture under capitalism.

The fascists' reactionary appeal to divide working people will need to be fought by putting forward instead the need for a common struggle by the oppressed and exploited regardless of nationality, ethnic background, or gender to throw off the rule of capitalists and landlords and begin building a more just and humane society.

But this battle will not take place solely within the realm of ideas.

As the social crisis deepens and a response among working people begins to develop, growing numbers of capitalists and their servants will resort to legal and extralegal measures to defend their class rule.

As these attacks escalate, they will need to be answered by working people fighting to defend their unions; by those fighting against racism, police brutality, and cop killings; by supporters of women's rights fighting to defend the right to abortion; by supporters of civil liberties fighting against attacks on democratic rights; by those standing up to capitalist environmental destruction; by those fighting anti-immigrant violence and deportations—in short, by all who struggle in the interests of the oppressed and exploited.

It is these activists and fighters who will be the ones most interested in studying the nature of fascism and the history of the struggle against it.

Many will find the Marxist perspective first outlined by Zetkin, and amplified subsequently by Leon Trotsky, Antonio Gramsci, and others, to be an essential weapon in the fight against the fascist threat.

In this context, growing numbers of working people and youth will be attracted to join in the fight for a socialist future.

That was the firm belief of Clara Zetkin.

In discussing fascism's appeal to youth, she pointed out that "the best of them are seeking an escape from deep anguish of the soul. They are longing for new and unshakable ideals and a world outlook that enables them to understand nature, society, and their own life; a world outlook that is not a sterile formula but operates creatively and constructively. Let us not forget that violent fascist gangs are not composed entirely of ruffians of war, mercenaries by choice, and venal lumpens who take pleasure in acts of terror. We also find among them the most energetic forces of these social layers, those most capable of development. We must go to them with conviction and understanding for their condition and their fiery longing, work among them, and show them a solution that does not lead backward but rather forward to communism. The overriding grandeur of communism as a world outlook will win their sympathies for us."

Fascism is ultimately a product of capitalist rule, Zetkin maintained. The threat of fascism will end once and for all only when the working class takes power out of the hands of the billionaire capitalist families and begins to build a new world.

Firmly convinced of this fact, Zetkin's unwavering confidence in the revolutionary potential of the working class can be seen at the conclusion of her 1923 report:

"Every single proletarian must feel like more than a mere wage slave, a plaything of the winds and storms of capitalism and of the powers that be. Proletarians must feel and understand themselves to be components of the revolutionary class, which will reforge the old state of the propertied into the new state of the soviet system. Only when we arouse revolutionary class consciousness in every worker and light the flame of class determination can we succeed in preparing and carrying out militarily the necessary overthrow of fascism. However brutal the offensive of world capital against the world proletariat may be for a time, however strongly it may rage, the proletariat will fight its way through to victory in the end."

§

About this volume

The two main documents in this book were presented to the Third Enlarged Plenum of the Communist International's Executive

Committee in June 1923. The entire proceedings of that plenum—including the discussion under Zetkin's report on fascism—can be found in *The Communist Movement at a Crossroads: Plenums of the Communist International's Executive Committee, 1922–1923*, edited by Mike Taber, to be published by the Historical Materialism Book Series for Brill and Haymarket Books. That volume is part of a series containing the proceedings of the first four congresses of the Comintern, which all took place while Lenin was still alive, as well as several other volumes of supplementary material.[5]

Zetkin's report and resolution to the Third Plenum contained in the present book have been translated by John Riddell from *Protokoll der Konferenz der Erweiterten Exekutive der Kommunistischen Internationale: Moskau, 12.-23. Juni 1923* (Hamburg: Verlag Carl Hoym Nachf., 1923). Subheads have been supplied by the editors.

Two appendices are also included:

1. The report and resolution by Zetkin to the international conference against war and fascism held in Frankfurt am Main, Germany, March 17–20, 1923. In the two documents presented to the conference by Zetkin, she outlined some of the ideas she returned to three months later at the Comintern's Executive Committee meeting.

   For this volume, translation of these documents was done from *Internationale Press-Korrespondenz*, no. 52 in 1923, by Sean Larson, who also helped edit the translation of Zetkin's report to the ECCI plenum.

2.   John Riddell's account of Zetkin's continued appeal for
     a united front against Nazism. Zetkin remained true to
     the united-front antifascist perspective that she outlined
     in 1923 even after the Communist Party turned its back
     on that approach. Her view was best summarized in her
     speech to the German Reichstag on August 30, 1932,
     with Hitler and the Nazis on the verge of power. Re-
     fusing to be silent in the face of a hostile audience, the
     seventy-four-year-old Zetkin called for a life-and-death
     battle against Nazism.

Zetkin's courageous call for antifascist action, issued less
than a year before her death, stands as a fitting tribute to her
lifetime of revolutionary struggle and to her legacy as a beacon
for future generations.

Mike Taber
John Riddell
January 2017

THE STRUGGLE
AGAINST FASCISM

Clara Zetkin

Fascism confronts the proletariat as an exceptionally dangerous and frightful enemy. Fascism is the strongest, most concentrated, and classic expression at this time of the world bourgeoisie's general offensive. It is urgently necessary that it be brought down. This is true not only with respect to the historic existence of the proletariat as a class, which will free humankind by surmounting capitalism. It is also a question of survival for every ordinary worker, a question of bread, working conditions, and quality of life for millions and millions of the exploited.

That is why the struggle against fascism must be taken up by the entire proletariat. It is evident that we will overcome this wily enemy all the sooner to the degree that we grasp its essential character and how that character is expressed. There has been great confusion regarding fascism, not only among the broad masses of proletarians but also within their revolutionary vanguard, among

Communists. At first, the prevailing view was that fascism was nothing more than violent bourgeois terror, and its character and effects were thought to be similar to those of the Horthy regime in Hungary.[1] Yet even though fascism and the Horthy regime employ the same bloody, terrorist methods, which bear down on the proletariat in the same way, the historical essence of the two phenomena is entirely different.

The terror in Hungary began after the defeat of an initially victorious revolutionary struggle. For a moment the bourgeoisie trembled before the proletariat's might. The Horthy terror emerged as revenge against the revolution. The agent of this revenge was a small caste of feudal officers.

Fascism is quite different from that. It is not at all the revenge of the bourgeoisie against the militant uprising of the proletariat. In historical terms, viewed objectively, fascism arrives much more as *punishment because the proletariat has not carried and driven forward the revolution that began in Russia.* And the base of fascism lies not in a small caste but in broad social layers, broad masses, reaching even into the proletariat. We must understand these essential differences in order to deal successfully with fascism. Military means alone cannot vanquish it, if I may use that term; we must also wrestle it to the ground politically and ideologically.

The social-democratic view of fascism

The view that fascism is merely a form of bourgeois terror, although advanced by some radical forces in our movement, is more characteristic of the outlook of many reformist social democrats. For them fascism is nothing but terror and violence—moreover a bourgeois reflex against the violence unleashed or threatened against bourgeois society by the proletariat. For the reformist gentlemen, the Russian Revolution plays the exact same role as biting into the apple of paradise plays for believers in the Bible. They view it as the origin of all expressions of terrorism in the present period. As if there had never been wars of imperialist piracy; as if there were no bourgeois class dictatorship! Thus fascism, for the reformists, is the consequence of the Russian Revolution—the proletariat's original sin in the Garden of Eden.

It was no less a figure than Otto Bauer who put forward the viewpoint in Hamburg that the Russian Communists and their co-thinkers carry special responsibility for present-day worldwide reaction by the bourgeoisie and for fascism; it is they who split parties and trade unions.[2] In making this bold assertion, Otto Bauer forgot that the notoriously harmless Independents [USPD] split from the [German] Social Democrats even before the Russian Revolution and its morally ruinous example. Bauer explains that world reaction, which reaches its highest point in fascism, is also caused in part by the fact that the Russian Revolution destroyed the Menshevik paradise in Georgia and Armenia.[3] He finds a third cause of world reaction in "Bolshevik terror" in general. In his remarks, however, he felt compelled to admit the following: "We in Central Europe are today obliged to confront the violent fascist organizations with the proletariat's defense guards. For we have no illusions that we can overcome direct violence through an appeal to democracy."

You would think that he would draw from this observation the conclusion that force must be met by force. However, reformist logic goes its own way, unfathomable, like the ways of heavenly providence.

Otto Bauer's concoction continues as follows: "I am not talking about methods that often do not lead to success, such as insurrection or even general strike. What is needed is coordination of parliamentary action with extra-parliamentary mass action."

Here Otto Bauer does not reveal to us the secret in his chaste political bosom as to what form of political action he favors in parliament and, even more, outside parliament. There are actions and then there are actions. There are parliamentary and mass actions that, from our point of view, consist of bourgeois rubbish, pardon my words. On the other hand, an action either inside or outside parliament can have a revolutionary character. Otto Bauer remains silent regarding the nature of the reformist actions. And the end product of his remarks on the struggle against world reaction is quite exceptional. It is unveiled as an international information bureau that will give precise reports on world reaction. Bauer explains: "The foundation of this International will possibly be met with skepticism. If we did not understand how to establish a news bureau that provides us with necessary information on reaction, this skepticism would be justified."

What lies behind this entire conception? It is the reformists' faith in the unshakable strength of the capitalist order and bourgeois class rule, along with distrust and cowardice toward the proletariat as a conscious and irresistible force of world revolution. The reformists view fascism as an expression of the unshakable and all-conquering power and strength of bourgeois class rule. The proletariat is not up to the task of taking up the struggle against it—that would be foolhardy and doomed to failure. So there is nothing left for the proletariat but to step aside quietly and modestly, and not provoke the tigers and lions of bourgeois class rule through a struggle for its liberation and its own rule. In short, the proletariat is to renounce all that for the present and future, and patiently wait to see whether a tiny bit can be gained through the route of democracy and reform.

The social roots of fascism

I have the opposite point of view, and so too, I'm sure, do all Communists. Specifically, we view fascism as an expression of the decay and disintegration of the capitalist economy and as a symptom of the bourgeois state's dissolution. We can combat fascism only if we grasp that it rouses and sweeps along broad social masses who have lost the earlier security of their existence and with it, often, their belief in social order. Fascism is rooted, indeed, in the dissolution of the capitalist economy and the bourgeois state. There were already symptoms of the proletarianization of bourgeois layers in prewar capitalism. The war shattered the capitalist economy down to its foundations. This is evident not only in the appalling impoverishment of the proletariat, but also in the proletarianization of very broad petty-bourgeois and middle-bourgeois masses, the calamitous conditions among small peasants, and the bleak distress of the "intelligentsia." The plight of the "intellectuals" is all the more severe given that prewar capitalism took measures to produce them in excess of demand. The capitalists wanted to extend the mass supply of labor power to the field of intellectual labor and thus unleash unbridled competition that would depress wages—excuse me, salaries. It was from these circles that imperialism recruited many of its ideological champions for the World War. At present all these layers are experiencing the collapse of the hopes they had placed in the war. Their conditions have become significantly worse. What weighs on them above all is the lack of security for their basic existence, which they still had before the war.

I base these conclusions not on conditions in Germany, where the bourgeois intellectuals face conditions of extreme impoverishment that are often more severe than the poverty of workers. No, look at Italy—which I will speak of shortly; the ruin of the economy there was decisive in causing social masses to join with fascism. Consider another country that, in contrast to other European states, emerged from the World War without severe convulsions: Britain. Just as much is said there today in the press and public life about the distress of the "new poor" as about the gigantic profits and luxury of the few "new rich." In the United States the farmers' movement responds to the growing plight of a large social layer. The conditions of the middle layers have worsened markedly in every country. In some countries this worsening leads to a point where these social layers are crushed or annihilated.

As a result there are countless thousands seeking new possibilities for survival, food security, and social standing. Their number is swelled by lower and mid-level government employees, the public servants. They are joined, even in the victor states, by former officers, noncoms, and the like, who now have neither employment nor profession. Social forces of this type offer fascism a contingent of distinguished figures who lend it in these countries a pronounced monarchist hue. But we cannot fully grasp the nature of fascism by viewing its evolution solely as a result of such economic pressures alone, which have been considerably enhanced by the financial crisis of the governments and their vanishing authority.

Failure of proletarian leadership

Fascism has another source. It is the blockage, the halting pace of world revolution resulting from betrayal by the reformist leaders of the workers' movement. Among a large part of the middle layers—the civil servants, bourgeois intellectuals, and the small and middle bourgeois—who were proletarianized or were threatened with that fate, the psychology of war was replaced by a degree of sympathy for reformist socialism. They hoped that, thanks to "democracy," reformist socialism could bring about global change. These expectations were painfully shattered. The reform socialists carried out a gentle coalition policy, whose costs were borne not only by proletarians and salaried workers but by civil servants, intellectuals, and lower and mid-level petty bourgeois of every type.

These layers lacked in general any theoretical, historical, or political education. Their sympathy for reform socialism was not deeply rooted. So as things turned out, they lost their belief not only in the reformist leaders but also in socialism itself. "The socialists promised an easing of our burdens and suffering, plus many beautiful things, and a reshaping of society on the foundations of justice and democracy," they said. "But the top dogs and the rich carry on and rule with even more severity than before." These bourgeois who were disappointed in socialism were joined by proletarian forces. All the disillusioned—whether bourgeois or proletarian in origin—nevertheless abandon a precious intellectual force that would enable them to look forward from the gloomy present to a bright and hopeful future. That force is trust in the proletariat as the class that will remake society. The betrayal by the reformist leaders does not weigh so heavily in the attitude of these disillusioned forces as another fact: namely, that the proletarian masses tolerate this betrayal, that they continue to accept the capitalist yoke without rebellion or resistance, indeed that they come to terms with a suffering even more bitter than before.

In addition, in order to be fair, I must add that the Communist parties as well, setting aside Russia, are not without responsibility for the fact that even within the proletariat there are disillusioned people who throw themselves into the arms of fascism. Quite frequently these parties' actions have been insufficiently vigorous, their initiatives lacking in scope, and their penetration of the masses inadequate. I set aside errors of policy that have led to defeats. There is no doubt that many of the most active, energetic, and revolutionary-minded proletarians have not found their way to us or have turned around on this path because they found us not energetic and aggressive enough. We have not succeeded in making them sufficiently aware of why we too, on some occasions, must hold back—even if unwillingly and with good cause.

Fascism's mass character

Masses in their thousands streamed to fascism. It became an asylum for all the politically homeless, the socially uprooted, the destitute and disillusioned. And what they no longer hoped for from the revolutionary proletarian class and from socialism, they now hoped would be achieved by the most able, strong, determined, and bold elements of every social class. All these forces must come together in a community. And this community, for the fascists, is the nation. They wrongly imagine that the sincere will to create a new and better social reality is strong enough to overcome all class antagonisms. The instrument to achieve fascist ideals is, for them, the state. A strong and authoritarian state that will be their very own creation and their obedient tool. This state will tower high above all differences of party and class, and will remake society in accord with their ideology and program.

It is evident that in terms of the social composition of its troops, fascism encompasses forces that can be extremely uncomfortable and even dangerous for bourgeois society. I'll go further and assert that these elements, if they come to understand their own best interests, *must* be dangerous for bourgeois society. Precisely! If this situation arises, then these forces must do what they can to ensure that bourgeois society is smashed as soon as possible and communism is achieved. But events up to now have nonetheless demonstrated that the revolutionary forces within fascism are outstripped and restrained by the reactionary forces.

What we see here is analogous to events in other revolutions. The petty-bourgeois and intermediate social forces at first vacillate indecisively between the powerful historical camps of the proletariat and bourgeoisie. They are induced to sympathize with the proletariat by their life's suffering and, in part, by their soul's noble longings and high ideals, so long as it is not only revolutionary in its conduct but also seems to have prospects for victory. Under the pressure of the masses and their needs and influenced by this situation, even the fascist leaders are forced to at least flirt with the revolutionary proletariat, even though they may not have any personal sympathy for it. But when it becomes clear that the proletariat itself has abandoned the goal of carrying the revolution further, that it is withdrawing from the battlefield under the influence of the reformist leaders, out of fear of revolution and respect for the capitalists—at this point the broad fascist masses find their way to the spot where most of their leaders were, consciously or unconsciously, from the very start: on the side of the bourgeoisie.

The bourgeoisie and fascism

The bourgeoisie naturally welcomes its new allies with joy. It sees in them a major increase in its power, a determined pack prepared for every form of violence in its service. The bourgeoisie, accustomed to rule, is unfortunately much more experienced and wise in judging the situation and defending its class interests than the proletariat, which is accustomed to the yoke. From the beginning the bourgeoisie has clearly grasped the situation and, thus, the advantage that it can draw from fascism. What does the bourgeoisie want? It is striving for the reconstruction of the capitalist economy, that is, the maintenance of its class domination. Under present circumstances, the precondition for achieving its goal is to considerably increase and intensify the exploitation and oppression of the working class.

The bourgeoisie is well aware that alone it does not possess the instruments of power to impose this fate on the exploited. Tormented by the scorpions of an upsurge in poverty, even the proletarian with the thickest skin finally begins to rebel against capitalism. The bourgeoisie can only conclude that over time, under such circumstances, even the mild and conciliatory sermons of the reform socialists will lose their dulling effect on the proletariat. It reckons that the proletariat can now be subjugated and exploited only through force. But the means of force available to the bourgeois state are beginning, in part, to break down. The state is losing the financial strength and moral authority needed to maintain blind loyalty and subjugation among its slaves. The bourgeoisie can no longer rely on its state's regular methods of force to secure its class rule. For that it needs an extralegal and nonstate instrument of force. That has been offered by the motley assemblage that makes up the fascist mob. That is why the bourgeoisie offers its hand for fascism's kiss, granting it complete freedom of action, contrary to all its written and un-written laws. It goes further. It nourishes fascism, maintains it, and promotes its development with all the means at its disposal in terms of political power and hoards of money.

It is evident that fascism has different characteristics in every country, based on specific circumstances. Nonetheless, in every country it has two essential features: a sham revolutionary program, which links up in extremely clever fashion with the moods, interests, and demands of broad social masses; and the use of brutal and violent terror.

Fascism's rise in Italy

The classic example of fascism's development and character today is Italy. Here fascism found its breeding ground in the disintegration and weakness of the economy. This might seem not to apply, given that Italy was among the victorious powers. Nonetheless, the war had a devastating impact on Italy's economy. The bourgeoisie returned from war victorious, but mortally wounded. The country's economic structure and development was decisive here. Only in northern Italy had a modern industrial capitalism emerged. In central and especially southern Italy, agrarian capital still reigned, to some extent still under feudal conditions, allied with a finance capitalism that had not yet scaled the heights of modern development and importance. Both were imperialist in orientation; both were hostile to the war; both gained little or nothing from the slaughter of millions. The noncapitalist peasantry suffered under them fearfully, and with it the urban petty bourgeoisie and proletariat. True, the artificially nourished heavy industry of northern Italy stashed away fabulous profits. Nonetheless, this industry lacked deep roots—Italy has neither coal nor iron—and its bloom soon faded.

All the evil effects of the war rained down on Italy's economy and governmental finances. A dreadful crisis unfolded. Industry, handicrafts, and trade ground to a halt; one bankruptcy followed another. The Banca di Sconto and the Ansaldo company, both creations of imperialism and war, collapsed. The war left behind hundreds of thousands searching for work and food, hundreds of thousands of cripples, widows, and orphans needing nourishment. The crisis augmented the army of those returning home in search of work and positions with crowds of laid-off working people, both men and women, both laborers and clerks. A massive wave of misery flooded through Italy, reaching its high point between the summer of 1920 and the spring of 1921. The industrial bourgeoisie of northern Italy, which had agitated so unscrupulously for war, was incapable of restoring the ruined economy. It did not have the political power to mobilize the state for its goals. It had lost control of the government, which fell back into the hands of the agrarian and financial capitalists under Giolitti's leadership. Even if that had not happened, the state, creaking in every joint, would not have possessed the means and opportunities to cope with the crisis and misery.

Thanks to this situation and in pace with its evolution, Italian fascism was able to sprout up. The predestined leader awaited in the person of Mussolini. In the autumn of 1914, Mussolini had been pacifist socialism's renegade. With the slogan "war or republic" he became the most fanatical of warmongers. In a daily paper founded with money from the Entente, *Il Popolo d'Italia*, he promised the masses of producers heaven on earth as the fruit of the war. Together with the industrial bourgeoisie he waded through the bloodbath of war; together with them he wanted to reshape Italy into a modern capitalist state. Mussolini had to woo the masses in order to be able to intervene as an active force in a situation that refuted all his prophecies and went counter to his goals. In 1919, he formed the first *fascio di combattenti* (league of frontline soldiers) in Milan, with the goal of assuring the survival and flourishing of the nation by "securing the revolutionary fruits of the revolutionary war for the heroes of the trenches and the working people." Fascist groups were formed in a number of cities. The new movement engaged from the start in a bitter struggle against the revolutionary workers' organizations, because these, Mussolini asserted, had "divided and weakened the nation" by putting forward a perspective of class struggle. Fascism also turned its spears against the Giolitti government, which it held to be wholly responsible for the horrific suffering of the period after the war. Fascism developed very slowly and weakly at first. It was still held back by the trust of the broad masses in socialism. In May 1920 there were in all of Italy only about one hundred fascist groups, none of them with more than twenty to thirty members.

Demoralization and terror

Soon fascism was able to draw nourishment and strength from a second major source. The objectively revolutionary situation led to the rise of a subjectively revolutionary mood in the Italian proletariat. The glorious example of the Russian workers and peasants had a strong influence here. In the summer of 1920, the metalworkers carried out the occupation of the factories.[4] Here and there, reaching into southern Italy, agricultural proletarians, small peasants, and tenant farmers occupied estates or rebelled in other ways against the large landowners. But this great historic moment found the workers' leaders to be feeble in spirit. The reformist leaders of the Socialist Party drew back in fear from the revolutionary perspective of broadening the factory occupation into a struggle for power. They forced the workers' struggle into the narrow confines of a purely economic movement, whose leadership was the business of the trade unions. In concord with D'Aragona and other officers of the General Confederation of Labor, they betrayed the rebellious wage slaves through a shameful compromise with the employers, benefiting from superb collaboration from the government, especially Giolitti. Leaders of the Socialist Party's left wing, from which the Communist Party later crystallized, still had too little training and experience to take command of the situation in thought and action and steer events in another direction. Moreover, the proletarian masses proved unable to go beyond their leaders and drive them forward in the direction of revolution.

The occupation of the factories ended in a severe defeat of the proletariat, causing discouragement, doubt, and timidity in its ranks. Thousands of workers turned their backs on the party and the trade unions. Many of them sank into indifference and mindlessness, while others joined bourgeois associations. Fascism won growing support among the disillusioned and also in the petty bourgeoisie and the bourgeois population. It had achieved victory politically and ideologically against a working class infected with reformism. In February 1921 there were about 1,000 fascists. Fascism won the masses through sham revolutionary demands advocated through unscrupulously demagogic agitation. Its pompous verbal radicalism was aimed above all against the government of Giolitti, "betrayer of the nation."

It was with fire and sword, however, that fascism proceeded against its second "enemy": the international workers' organizations, the enemies of the fatherland. Mussolini demanded, in keeping with his republican, antimonarchist, and imperialist views, the dismissal of the royal dynasty and the literal beheading of Giolitti. His followers began to "discipline" the "antinationals," that is, class-conscious workers' organizations, with direct, bloody terror. In the spring of 1921 the fascists undertook their first "punitive expeditions." They struck out against the rural proletarians, whose organizational headquarters were devastated and burned out and whose leaders were murdered. Only later did the fascist terror extend to the proletarians of the large cities. The prosecutors let all this take place without regard to law and justice. The bourgeoisie, whether industrial or agrarian, openly sponsored fascist terrorism, supporting it with money and in other ways. Even though the workers' occupation of the factories ended in defeat, the bourgeoisie feared a future revival of proletarian power. In the municipal elections, the Socialists had won a third of the 8,000 councils. Preventive action was necessary. To be sure!

Fascist electoral gains

The government then had cause and opportunity to forcibly strike down fascism, which was moving in on it threateningly. But in the prevailing situation, that would have caused a strengthening of the workers' movement. Better the fascists than the Socialists and revolutionaries, Giolitti thought. The sly old fox dissolved parliament and decreed new elections in May 1921. He created an "alliance for order" of all the bourgeois parties and brought into it the fascist organizations. During the electoral campaign, fascism engaged in boisterous republican appeals. This antimonarchical and antidynastic agitation fell silent now that the Agrarian Party leaders and masses were joining it. The fascist gains in the election were largely due to this support as well as the extension and growing strength of the *fasci*, which in May 1921 had 2,000 groups. Mussolini was indisputably exposing himself and his cause to the risk inherent in flooding the fascist movement with agrarian forces. He recognized that, by halting sham revolutionary antimonarchical agitation, he was giving up a strong incentive for the masses to join the fascists.

When the electoral battle was over, Mussolini wanted to go back to his slogans of 1919. In an interview with a reporter from *Giornale d'Italia*—which represents the interests of heavy industry—he stated that the elected fascists would not take part in the opening of parliament because it was impossible for them to shout, "Long live the king!" after the speech from the throne. This announcement had the effect of showing the strength of the agrarian wing in fascism. Some deputies elected with support of the fascist groups quit to join the monarchists and nationalists. A meeting was called of the fascist deputies together with regional delegates of the *fasci* in order to settle the dispute. Mussolini and his proposal were defeated. He reined in his republicanism with the explanation that he did not want to split fascism over this question.

Fascist apparatus

This defeat prompted Mussolini to set about constituting fascism as an organized and centralized party; until then it had been only a loose movement. The transformation took place at the first fascist congress in November 1921. While Mussolini won on this point, he was defeated in the selection of the party leadership; he did not have it fully under his control. His personal supporters made up only one half; the other half were monarchist Agrarians. This situation is significant. It indicates a conflict within fascism that has continued and intensified up to the present day, a conflict that will contribute to fascism's decay. It is the conflict between agrarian and industrial capital or, in political terms, between monarchists and republicans. The party now has 500,000 members.

Constituting fascism as a party was not enough in itself to grant Mussolini the power to become master of the working class and to compel the proletariat, through even more dismal drudgery, to contribute to the reconstruction and further development of the capitalist economy. For this purpose he needed a dual apparatus. One apparatus to corrupt the workers, and another to suppress them with armed force and terrorist means.

The apparatus to corrupt the workers' movement was created by founding the fascist unions, named "national corporations." They were to carry out systematically what fascism had done from the start: combat the revolutionary workers' movement, indeed every independent movement of the workers. Mussolini always rejects the charge that he is conducting a struggle against the working class. He continually gives assurances that he wants to raise the working class materially and culturally and not lead it backwards into "the harrowing conditions of a slave-like existence." But all that must be in the framework of the "nation" and subordinated to its interests; the class struggle is sharply rejected.

The fascist trade unions were founded with the explicit goal of providing an antidote against not only the revolutionary organizations of the proletariat but also against class organizations of any kind. Every proletarian class organization is immediately suspected by Mussolini and his henchmen of being revolutionary in character. Mussolini created his own trade unions, encompassing all workers, employees, and employers in a given trade or industry. Some of the organized employers have declined to join Mussolini's unions, as has the agricultural league and the league of industrialists. Nonetheless, despite their heresy, they are not called to account by fascist punitive expeditions. These forays take place only where proletarians are concerned, who perhaps are not even in the revolutionary movement but nonetheless struggle in accordance with their class interests. Tens of thousands of workers have been forced to join the fascist unions, which are said to include about 800,000 members.

The fascist groups for terrorist subjugation of the working class in Italy are the so-called squadrons. These constitute a military organization that has evolved out of the agrarian punitive expeditions. Bands of "punishers," which here and there formed spontaneously, became permanent organizations of paid mercenaries, who carry out terror as a profession. The squadrons developed over time into a purely military force, one that carried out the coup and underpins Mussolini's dictatorial power. After the seizure of power and the establishment of the fascist state they were legalized as a "national militia," a part of the bourgeois state. They are committed, as was officially declared, "to the service of God, the nation, and the prime minister"—please note: not the king. There are various estimates of their strength. At the time of the fascist coup[5] they numbered between 100,000 and 300,000; now they are half a million.

The failed general strike

Just as the failure and betrayal of the reformist leaders helped give birth to fascism, so too fascism's conquest of state power was preceded by yet another reformist betrayal and therewith also another defeat of the Italian proletariat. On July 31, [1922] a secret session took place of the Italian reformist workers' leaders—from both unions and the [Socialist] party; Turati was there, just like D'Aragona. It decided to proclaim a general strike through the General Confederation of Labor on August 1, a strike that was not prepared and not organized.[6] As things stood, it could end only in a dreadful defeat for the proletariat. In many localities the strike began only after it had already collapsed elsewhere. This was a defeat just as great and fateful as the occupation of the factories had been. It gave courage to the fascists for their coup, while discouraging and demoralizing the workers so that, passive and hopeless, they refrained from further resistance and let everything happen. After the coup the betrayal of the reformist leaders was sealed when Baldesi, one of the most influential leaders of the Italian trade-union confederation and the Socialist Party, declared on orders of Mussolini that he was ready to join the fascist government. This shameful alliance collapsed—what a disgrace—not because of the reformists' opposition and protest, but because of the resistance of the fascist Agrarians.

Comrades! This short overview will have enabled you to recognize the interconnection in Italy between the development of fascism and the economic decay that impoverished and deluded the masses; between the development of fascism and the betrayal of the reformist leaders—cowards who abandoned the proletarians in the struggle. The weaknesses of the Communist Party also played a role here. Quite apart from its numerical weakness, the party surely also made a policy error in viewing fascism solely as a military phenomenon and overlooking its ideological and political side. Let us not forget that before beating down the proletariat through acts of terror, fascism in Italy had already won an ideological and political victory over the workers' movement that lay at the root of its triumph. It would be very dangerous to fail to consider the importance of overcoming fascism ideologically and politically.

Fascist promises vs. performance

It is evident that, in terms of its organization and strength, fascism could evolve in the way briefly outlined here only because it had a program that was very attractive to the broad masses. We face a question that is important to proletarians of every country: What has fascism in Italy done since taking power to realize its program? What is the nature of the state that is its chosen instrument? Has it shown itself to be the promised state standing above class and party, granting justice to every layer of society? Or has it shown itself to be a tool of the propertied minority and especially of the industrial bourgeoisie? This is best judged by comparing the most important demands of the fascist program with the way they have been implemented.

What did fascism promise, in political terms, when it stormed in like Samson with wild, flowing hair?

A reform of the right to vote and consistently implemented proportional representation. What do we see? The old and flawed proportional representation law of 1919 is to be repealed and replaced by an electoral law that is a joke, a bloody mockery of proportional representation. The party that gets the most votes is to receive two-thirds of the seats in parliament. There has been a debate on whether it should be two-thirds or three-quarters. According to recent press reports, the fascists will be content for the strongest party—namely their own—to get two-thirds, and the remaining third to be distributed proportionally among the various other parties. That's some electoral reform!

Mussolini promised women the right to vote and to be elected. Recently an international bourgeois conference for women's suffrage met in Rome.[7] Mussolini graciously honored the women by his presence and explained to them with a sweet smile that women would obtain the right to vote—but only for the municipal councils. Political rights would thus still be denied them. Moreover, not all women would gain rights in municipal elections; only those who could give evidence of a certain level of education, plus women with "war medals," and women whose husbands possessed a sufficiently large bag of money to pay a certain level of taxes. That's how he keeps his promise with regard to equal rights for women.

Fascism included in its program the abolition of the senate and the creation of an economic parliament, standing alongside the political one. We hear nothing more about the economic parliament. But when Mussolini made his first address to the senate, that junk room of all reactionaries, he celebrated its magnificent contributions in the past and confirmed its great achievements in the present—all of which required an enhancement of the senate's influence in lawmaking.

The fascist program called for immediate summoning of a national assembly to reform the constitution. Where does that stand? Not a word has been said about this assembly. On the contrary, constitutional reform looks like this: the parliament—made up as I have described, which means fascism as its majority party—proposes a prime minister. The proposed fascist prime minister must then be affirmed by the king. The prime minister puts together his government any way he wants, presents himself and his cabinet to the parliament, and receives a vote of confidence, after which parliament leaves the scene, adjourned for four years—that is, for the entire period of its term in office.

Let us also compare the fascists' promises in the social sphere with their performance. Fascism promised legal protections for the eight-hour day and the establishment of a minimum wage for both industrial and agricultural workers. The law now proposed on the eight-hour day has a hundred exceptions and concludes with a provision that it can also be set aside in some cases. What is more, the eight-hour day has already vanished in practice for broad layers of the proletariat, especially for railway workers, postal employees, and other communications and transport employees, for whom—exactly on the model of "that miserable dog Groener"[8]—eight hours spent on-call at work is replaced by eight hours of work actually performed.

What is the situation regarding the establishment of a minimum wage? Thanks to the terrorist shackling and destruction of the trade unions, thanks to the conduct of fascist "corporations" pledged to "civil peace," the employers' resistance against wage demands has been so reinforced that workers have been unable, given the bad economic situation, to defend even their previous wage levels. Wage reductions of 20–30 percent on average have taken place—50 percent for a great many workers.

Indeed, there are even cases where the wage reduction comes to 60 percent.

Fascism talked about insurance for the elderly and for invalids, which would shield them against the worst levels of poverty and suffering. And what happened to this promise? The very weak beginnings of social welfare for the elderly, infirm, and sick, which took the form of a fund of 50 million lire, have been abolished. The 50 million lire was simply stricken from the budget "to save money," so that those suffering from poverty no longer have access to any welfare provisions. Also stricken from the budget are the 50 million lire for employment agencies and support to the unemployed, and 60 million lire for the cooperative credit unions.

Fascism had raised the demand that workers take part in the technical leadership of the factory—in other words, control of production. It was promised that fascism would subject public enterprises to the technical supervision of factory councils. Now a law is being considered that simply abolishes the factory councils. Further, public enterprises are to be handed over to be operated by private employers, and this has already been done in part. The manufacture of matches, previously a state monopoly, has now wound up in the hands of private profiteers. So too have the postal package business, the telephone industry, the radio-telegram business, and also the railways. Mussolini has stated that the fascists are "liberals in the classic meaning of the word."

Let us consider some of the fruits of fascism in the financial field. Fascism promised a thorough tax reform. Their "authoritarian" state was to use its power to levy a general and strongly progressive tax on capital, which was supposed to be, to some extent, an "expropriation of capital." But what followed was the elimination of various taxes on luxury goods, such as on carriages, automobiles, and the like. In justification, it is said that such taxes "restrict national production and destroy property and the family." In addition, it is now planned to expand indirect taxes, with an equally fanciful justification, namely that extending these taxes would reduce consumption and thus promote exports abroad. Moreover, the requirement for securities to be held in the name of their owner—the so-called "nominality of securities"—has been eliminated, opening wide the door to tax evaders.

Mussolini and his cronies called for confiscation of church assets. Instead of that, the fascist government has brought back into effect a number of old and long-ago-terminated concessions to the clergy. Religious instruction in the schools was abolished fifty years ago; Mussolini has brought it back, and a crucifix must now hang in every school.

Fascism had demanded that government contracts for war supplies be modified and that up to 85 percent of war profits pass over to the government. What happened? Parliament set up a commission to review the contracts for war supplies. It was supposed to present a report to the parliament as a whole. Doing this would no doubt have deeply compromised most of the captains of heavy industry, the patrons and benefactors of fascism. One of Mussolini's first decisions was that this commission would report only to him personally, and that anyone revealing anything of the report's contents would be punished with six months' imprisonment. As for seizing war profits, on this point all the fascist trumpets fell silent, while billions were approved for heavy industry to cover deliveries of various types.

Fascism also wanted to fundamentally overhaul the armed forces. It demanded abolition of the standing army, a short period of service, limitation of the army to defense of the country as opposed to engaging in imperialist wars, and so on. How was this program carried out? The standing army was not abolished. The time of compulsory service was raised from eight months to eighteen months, which enlarged the 250,000-man army to 350,000. True, the Guardia Regia, a sort of militarily armed and organized police, was abolished. Was this perhaps because it was quite unpopular with the people, and especially the workers, after it had intervened in assemblies, strikes, and the like? Quite the contrary! Mussolini considered it too "democratic" because it answered to the ministry of the interior rather than to the general staff, and Mussolini feared that these forces could come into conflict with his squadrons and act against him.

The Guardia Regia had included 35,000 police. To make up for it, the size of the Carabinieri was increased from 65,000 to 90,000. In addition, the number of police was doubled—even the detectives and the customs police. In addition, the fascist government converted the "blackshirt" squadrons into a national militia. Their number was initially estimated at 100,000, but a recent decision in the fascist camp will raise it in the future to half a million.

The squadrons were infiltrated by the nationalist "blueshirts" —agrarian-monarchist forces—a fact that must have made

Mussolini tremble with fear of an uprising against his dictatorship. From the moment when the squadrons first appeared, he took measures to place them under the political leadership of the party, that is, subject to his supremacy. He believed that goal to have been achieved by placing the squadrons under a national supreme command chosen by the party leadership. But the political leadership could not prevent conflicts within the squadrons, conflicts that became increasingly sharp when the nationalists, the "blueshirts," entered the squadrons. In order to break their influence, Mussolini arranged for a decision that obligated every party member to join the national militia, so that its strength became equal to that of the party. Mussolini hoped in this way to politically subdue the agrarian forces that were resisting him. Nonetheless, bringing party members into the militia will embed the political conflicts in it, and these conflicts will develop further there until they lead to decay.

The armed forces were to serve only to defend the fatherland. That was the promise. But the burgeoning size of the army and the enormous scope of armaments are oriented to major imperialist adventures. The artillery has been enormously expanded, the size of the officer corps has increased, and the navy is receiving special support. A large number of cruisers, torpedo destroyers, submarines, and the like are on order. The air force is developing in an especially conspicuous fashion. Orders have already gone out for 1,000 new planes, and many airfields have been built. The air force has its own commission, and hundreds of millions of lire have been approved for heavy industry to build the most modern machines and murderous instruments of death.

When one compares the program of Italian fascism with its actual implementation, one thing becomes evident: the complete ideological bankruptcy of the movement. There is a blatant contradiction between what fascism promised and what it delivered to the masses. All the talk about how the fascist state will place the interests of the nation above everything, once exposed to the wind of reality, burst like a soap bubble. The "nation" revealed itself to be the bourgeoisie; the ideal fascist state revealed itself to be the vulgar, unscrupulous bourgeois class state. This ideological bankruptcy must lead sooner or later to political bankruptcy.

Fascism's contradictions

And that day is now approaching. Fascism is incapable of holding together even the different bourgeois currents with whose silent and beneficent patronage it came to power. Fascism wanted to secure the power for social rebirth by seizing control of the state and utilizing its apparatus of power for its own ends. It has not even succeeded in fully subduing the bureaucratic apparatus. A sharp struggle has broken out between the old entrenched bureaucracy and the new fascist officials. The same antagonism exists between the old regular army with its officer corps and the fascist militia with its new leaders. The conflict between fascism and the bourgeois parties is growing.

Mussolini had a plan to create a unified class organization of the bourgeoisie in the shape of the fascist party as the counterpart of the revolutionary proletariat. That is why he devoted so much effort to smashing or absorbing all the bourgeois parties. He succeeded in absorbing one single party, the nationalists.[9] As we have seen, there are many indications that this fusion is two-sided. The attempt to unify the bourgeois, liberal, republican, and democratic groups in a conservative framework failed miserably. Quite the contrary: fascist policies have led the remnants of bourgeois democracy to draw on their previous ideology. Confronted with Mussolini's drive for power and use of violence, they have taken up a struggle "to defend the constitution and restore the old bourgeois liberty."

Fascism's incapacity to consolidate and deepen its hold on political power is well illustrated by its relationship to the Catholic People's Party,[10] indisputably the largest and most influential bourgeois party in Italy. Mussolini counted on being successful in breaking away this party's agrarian right wing and unifying it with the fascists, while thereby weakening the left wing and securing its dissolution. Things worked out differently. At the recent congress of the *populari* in Turin, there was a true outcry against fascism. Those on the party's right wing who tried to speak favorably and protectively of fascism were shouted down. The most severe criticisms of its policies, by contrast, were met with enthusiastic agreement.

Behind these conflicts—those I have mentioned and others—is the class conflict that cannot be talked out of existence by organizational maneuvers and sermons about civil peace. Class contradictions are mightier than all the ideologies that deny their existence, and these contradictions find expression despite fascism, indeed thanks to fascism and against it. The conduct of the *populari* reflects the awareness of broad layers of urban petty bourgeois and small peasants regarding their status as a class and their antagonisms to large-scale capital. This is extraordinarily important with regard to the fascists' hold on power in Italy, or more properly, for the disintegration that it is headed toward. These layers, and especially the women within them, are deeply influenced by Catholicism and the church. Mussolini has therefore done all he could to win the Vatican. But the Vatican has not dared to counter the first stages of antifascist rebellion among the peasant masses in the People's Party.

The small peasants see that fascism brings the bourgeoisie lower taxes, increased possibilities for tax evasion, and fat contracts. Meanwhile, the small peasants feel the weight of heavier taxes through indirect payments and notably through a recalculation of agricultural income. The same holds true for the petty-bourgeois masses in the city. They are provoked into sharp opposition by triumphant fascism's abolition of rent control; landlords once again have unlimited power to impose high rents. The growing rebellion of small peasants and agricultural workers finds pointed expression precisely in the rural regions where fascism imagined its squadrons to have broken all resistance. For example, in Boscoreale near Naples more than a thousand peasants stormed the town hall in protest against oppressive taxes. In three localities in Novara province, the agricultural workers were able to assert with success their previous wages and working conditions. They did this by occupying a number of estates, indeed with the support of fascist squadrons. It is evident that the idea of class struggle is beginning to sink roots even within the ranks of fascism.

Proletarian awakening

Of particular importance is the awakening of sections of the proletariat that were intoxicated and poisoned by fascism. Meanwhile, fascism is incapable of defending the workers' interests
against the bourgeoisie, and incapable of keeping the promises
that it made, particularly to the fascist trade unions. The greater
its victories, the more incapable it is of posing as the proletariat's
protector. Fascism cannot even force the employers to hold to fascist promises about the advantages of common organizations.[11]
Wherever only a few workers are organized in the fascist trade
unions, it may be possible for a capitalist to pay better wages to
these few. But wherever the masses are herded into the fascist
organizations, the employers do not take into consideration the
"fascist brothers," because it would cost too much—and where
moneybags and profits are concerned, capitalist gentlemen do
not display kindliness.

The awakening of the proletarians has been speeded up in
particular by the large number of workers thrown into the street
with no sustenance, not only in private concerns but also in
public enterprises. Soon after the fascist coup, 17,000 railway
workers were laid off. Further layoffs followed and more are defi-
nitely in store. The governmental army workshops were closed,
leaving 24,000 workers with no income and delivered over to
unrestricted exploitation in the private workshops.

A fervent rebellion against fascist economic policies is
emerging precisely among the workers organized by the fascists
themselves. In Turin, Naples, Trieste, Venice, and a large num-

ber of other cities it was the fascist trade unions that took the lead without exception in joining with workers of other parties and organizations—including the Communist and syndicalist workers—in a massive public rally against the layoffs and workshop closures. Several hundred war invalids who had been dismissed from the army workshops traveled from Naples to Rome in order to protest the injustice they had suffered. They hoped Mussolini himself would grant them justice and protection, and instead, as reward for their faith, they were arrested the moment they got off the trains. The dockworkers of Monfalcone and Trieste, the workers of many localities and industries—all of them members of fascist organizations—have moved into action. In some places factory occupations have once again come about, carried out in fact by workers in fascist unions, with sympathetic toleration or support by the squadrons.

These facts show that ideological bankruptcy leads to political bankruptcy, and that it will be the workers above all who will quickly begin thinking once again in terms of their class interests and responsibilities.

Who will topple fascism?

There are many conclusions to be drawn. First, we must not view fascism as a homogenous phenomenon, as a block of granite, against which all our efforts will shatter. Fascism is contradictory by nature, encompassing different conflicting forces that will lead it to internal decay and disintegration. We must take up the struggle more energetically not only for the souls of proletarians that have fallen to fascism but for those of small and medium bourgeois, small peasants, intellectuals—in a word, all the layers that are placed today, by their economic and social position, in increasingly sharp conflict with large-scale capitalism.

However, it would be extremely dangerous to assume that the ideological and political decay in Italy will lead quickly to military collapse. True, fascism's military decay and collapse will come—it must come—but this may be a lengthy drawn-out process because of the inertia of the available instruments of power. The proletariat in Italy will break free of fascism. It will again grow conscious, stronger, and more purposeful in the struggle for its interests. It will take up again the revolutionary class struggle for its freedom. But during this process, the Italian comrades and the proletariat must reckon with the fact that fascism, while perishing ideologically and politically, will assail them with military terrorism, with unsparing and unscrupulous violence. We must be prepared! A monster, even in its death throes, often succeeds in dealing out devastating blows. For that reason the revolutionary proletarians, Communists, and Socialists must follow the path of class struggle, prepared and armed for harsh battles.

The worst thing we could do would be to allow our historical understanding of fascism to sway us toward inactivity, toward waiting, or toward the postponement of arming ourselves and struggling against fascism. Yes, fascism is surely condemned to decay internally and to fall apart. Only temporarily can it serve the bourgeoisie as a tool of class struggle; only temporarily can it reinforce, whether legally or illegally, the power of the bourgeois state against the proletariat. Still, it would be disastrous for us to fall into the role of clever and refined observers of this process of decay. On the contrary, it is our bounden duty to drive this process forward and hasten it by every possible means.

Fascism in Germany

Such is the special duty of the proletariat not only in Italy, where this process will probably take place first; *it is also the task of the German proletariat.* Fascism is an international phenomenon; we all agree on that. Thus far, next to Italy, its strength is greatest in Germany. Here the war's outcome and the failure of the revolution have been favorable for its growth. That is understandable, bearing in mind what we know regarding the roots of fascism.

In Germany, the economy has been especially devastated by the lost war, the burden of reparations, and the Versailles Treaty.[12] The state is shattered down to its roots. The government is weak, without authority, a plaything in the hands of Stinnes and his cronies.[13] In my opinion, there is no country where conflicts are so great as in Germany between the objectively mature conditions for revolution and the subjective immaturity of the proletariat, as a result of the betrayals, the outlook, and the conduct of the reformist leaders. Nowhere did Social Democracy collapse so shamefully when the war broke out as in Germany. Here capitalist industry was highly developed; here the proletariat could be proud of its strong organization and lengthy Marxist schooling. We can concede that the British, French, and Austrian Social-Democratic parties and all the organizations united in the Second International had their strong points. But the leading party, the model party, was the German Social Democratic Party. Its breakdown is therefore a more unforgivable and outrageous crime than the breakdown of other workers' parties. There are more grounds to excuse or forgive the collapse of the other parties when the war broke out than there are for the German Social Democratic Party. The impact of this collapse recoiled on the proletarian masses in a particularly strong and destructive fashion. When German imperialism was shattered by Entente imperialism, the preconditions here were particularly favorable for fascism to shoot up rapidly.

But despite everything, I am convinced that the Versailles Treaty and the occupation of the Ruhr[14] with all its deeds of violence have not promoted fascism in Germany as much as Mussolini's coup. That coup gave a bigger boost to the German fascists than any other event. It gave them self-confidence and faith in their victory. The defeat and collapse of fascism in Italy would immediately deal the greatest blow of demoralization to fascists in Germany, and would greatly encourage the proletariat. All the more so if the proletariat can say: Fascism in Italy was victorious and for a while enjoyed the height of power, but now it is no more, not only because it had to be torn apart by its internal contradictions, but also because of the strong and purposeful action of the proletarian masses there. This understanding would spread internationally, whatever the situation in individual countries.

So it is our duty internationally to work with all our power to overcome fascism in Italy. But in this effort, we must not forget that there is a precondition for successfully overcoming fascism abroad, and that is for us to also combat organized fascism in our own country with all our strength and thoroughly defeat it.

I have outlined the development of fascism in Italy rather fully—although far from fully enough—because it is mature, clearly defined, and complete before our eyes. The Italian comrades will fill out my remarks. I am not going to portray fascism in other countries; this can be done by delegates of our parties in these countries.

Combating fascism's appeal

In the resolution I have proposed, various methods are outlined for us to employ, various tasks that we have to carry out, in order to win mastery over fascism. I will not discuss the resolution in detail; I believe it speaks for itself. I only want to stress that these tasks run along two lines. One group of tasks aims at overcoming fascism ideologically and politically. This task is enormously important. It demands to a certain extent a rethinking or a more precise evaluation of some social phenomena that are peculiar to fascism in its essence. Also, it demands intense activity. We must remain aware that, as I said at the outset, fascism is a movement of the hungry, the suffering, the disappointed, and those without a future. We must make efforts to address the social layers that are now lapsing into fascism and either incorporate them in our struggles or at least neutralize them in the struggle. We must employ clarity and force to prevent them from providing troops for the bourgeois counterrevolution. To the extent that we do not win such layers for our party and our ideals and are unable to incorporate them into the rank and file of the struggling revolutionary proletarian battle forces, we must succeed in neutralizing them, sterilizing them, or whatever word you want to use. They must no longer threaten us as warriors for the bourgeoisie. The preconditions for our success are present in the living conditions that bourgeois class rule imposes on these layers in this stage of historical development.

In my view, it is extremely important that we purposefully and consistently carry out the ideological and political struggle for the souls of those in these layers, including the bourgeois intelligentsia. We must understand that, incontestably, growing masses here are seeking an escape route from the dreadful suffering of our time. This involves much more than filling one's stomach. No, the best of them are seeking an escape from deep anguish of the soul. They are longing for new and unshakable ideals and a world outlook that enables them to understand nature, society, and their own life; a world outlook that is not a sterile formula but operates creatively and constructively. Let us not forget that violent fascist gangs are not composed entirely of ruffians of war, mercenaries by choice, and venal lumpens who take pleasure in acts of terror. We also find among them the most energetic forces of these social layers, those most capable of development. We must go to them with conviction and understanding for their condition and their fiery longing, work among them, and show them a solution that does not lead backward but rather forward to communism. The overriding grandeur of communism as a world outlook will win their sympathies for us.

To the masses!

In contrast to the Second International, the Comintern is not an International for the elite of white proletarians of Europe and America. It is an International for the exploited of all races. Thus the Communist Party of each country must now be not just a vanguard fighter for wageworkers in the narrow sense of the term, not only a tribune of the interests of proletarians engaged in manual labor, but also a champion of intellectual workers, a leader of all social layers whose vital interests and whose longing to attain a more advanced culture places them in growing contradiction to the capitalist order. I therefore gladly welcome the decision of our plenum to take up the struggle for a workers' and peasants' government. The new slogan is not only irrefutably applicable to the largely agrarian countries of the Balkans like Bulgaria, Romania, and so on; it is also of great significance for Italy, France, Germany, and especially the United States. The slogan is virtually a requirement for the struggle to defeat fascism. It requires that we go among the broadest layers of exploited peasant producers and agricultural workers and bring them the joyful message of liberating communism. The task is to show all social layers in which fascism is recruiting a mass following that we Communists defend their interests through intense activity against bourgeois class rule.

There is something else we must do. We must not limit ourselves to struggle with and for the masses with our political and economic program. True, the political and economic demands press their way to the fore. But how can we offer the masses more than just defense of their bread? We must at the same time bring them the entire noble inner substance of communism as a world outlook. If that is done, our movement will sink roots in all social layers, and especially among bourgeois intellectuals whom recent historical developments have rendered insecure in their thinking and their striving, who have lost their old world outlook without being able to find a new one in the turmoil of these times. Let us ensure that these seekers do not go astray.

In the spirit of this line of thought, I say, "To the masses!" But let me underline a precondition for success. We must not forget the words of Goethe, "*Getretener Quark wird breit, nicht stark.*"[15] We must maintain our Communist ideology in all its strength and clarity. The more we go to the masses, the more necessary it is for the Communist Party to be organizationally and ideologically unified. We cannot pour ourselves out broadly like a puddle dissolving into the masses. That would lead to damaging opportunism, and our efforts among the masses would collapse in humiliating defeat. If we make concessions to the masses' "lack of understanding"—and I mean both the old and the new masses—we then abandon our true vocation as a party. We lose what is most important for the seekers—that which binds them together: the flame of a new social life that warms and illuminates, bringing hope and strength in the struggle.

What we need is to reshape our agitation and propagandistic methods and our literature in line with these new tasks. If the mountain will not come to Mohammad, Mohammad has no choice but to go to the mountain. If the new masses that we must attract do not come to us, we must find them and talk to them in their own language, one corresponding to how they see things, without giving up the slightest bit of our Communist outlook. We need special literature for agitation among the peasantry, special literature for civil servants and the small and middle bourgeois of every type, and also literature devoted to work among intellectuals. Let us not underestimate the role that intellectuals can play not only in the revolution but also after the revolution. Let us recall the extraordinarily damaging sabotage carried out by intellectuals in Russia after the November [1917] revolution. We want to learn from the experiences of our Russian brothers. This is why we must understand that it is far from unimportant whether intellectuals are with us or against us, both at the moment of revolution and after it takes place.

Workers' self-defense and the united front

Thus the struggle against fascism imposes on us a rich array of new tasks. Every single section of the Communist International has the duty of taking up these tasks and carrying them out in a manner corresponding to the specific conditions in their country.

And we must be aware that overcoming fascism ideologically and politically is not in itself sufficient to protect the struggling proletariat from the malice and violence of this enemy.

At present the proletariat has urgent need for self-defense against fascism, and this self-protection against fascist terror must not be neglected for a single moment. At stake is the proletarians' personal safety and very existence; at stake is the survival of their organizations. Proletarian self-defense is the need of the hour. We must not combat fascism in the way of the reformists in Italy, who beseeched them to "leave me alone, and then I'll leave you alone." On the contrary! Meet violence with violence. But not violence in the form of individual terror—that will surely fail. But rather violence as the power of the revolutionary organized proletarian class struggle.

We have already made a start here in Germany toward the organized self-protection of the working class against fascism by forming the factory detachments.[16] These self-defense units need to be expanded and imitated in other countries as a basis for international success against fascism.

But proletarian struggle and self-defense against fascism requires a proletarian united front. Fascism does not ask if the worker in the factory has a soul painted in the white and blue colors of Bavaria; or is inspired by the black, red, and gold colors of the bourgeois republic; or by the red banner with a hammer and sickle. It does not ask whether the worker wants to restore the Wittelsbach dynasty [of Bavaria], is an enthusiastic fan of Ebert, or would prefer to see our friend Brandler as president of the German Soviet Republic. All that matters to fascism is that they encounter a class-conscious proletarian, and then they club him to the ground. That is why workers must come together for struggle without distinctions of party or trade-union affiliation.

Proletarian self-defense against fascism is one of the strongest forces driving to establish and strengthen the proletarian united front. Without the united front it is impossible for the proletariat to carry out self-defense successfully. It is therefore necessary to expand our agitation in the factories and deepen it. Our efforts must overcome above all the indifference and the lack of class consciousness and solidarity in the soul of the workers, who say, "Let the others struggle and take action; it's not my business." We must pound into every proletarian the conviction that it *is* their business. "Don't leave me out. I must be there. Victory is in sight."

Every single proletarian must feel like more than a mere wage slave, a plaything of the winds and storms of capitalism and of the powers that be. Proletarians must feel and understand themselves to be part of the revolutionary class, which will reforge the old state of the propertied into the new state of the soviet system. Only when we arouse revolutionary class consciousness in every worker and light the flame of class determination can we succeed in preparing and carrying out militarily the necessary overthrow of fascism. However brutal the offensive of world capital against the world proletariat may be for a time, however strongly it may rage, the proletariat will fight its way through to victory in the end. Despite fascism, we see the capitalist economy, the bourgeois state, and class rule at the end of their tether. Symptoms of fascist decay and disintegration in bourgeois society speak to us loudly and piercingly of coming victory, provided that the proletariat struggles with knowledge and will in a united front. That's what must be!

Above the chaos of present conditions, the giant form of the proletariat will rear up with the cry: "I have the will! I have the power! I am the struggle and the victory! The future belongs to me!"

RESOLUTION ON FASCISM

This resolution, authored by Zetkin, was adopted on June 23, 1923, by the Third Enlarged Plenum of the Executive Committee of the Communist International.

Fascism is a characteristic symptom of decay in this period, an expression of the ongoing dissolution of the capitalist economy and the decomposition of the bourgeois state.

Fascism is rooted above all in the impact of the imperialist war and the heightened and accelerated dislocation of the capitalist economy that it caused among broad layers of the small and middle bourgeoisie, the small peasantry, and the "intelligentsia." This process dashed the hopes of these layers by demolishing their previous conditions of life and the degree of security they had previously enjoyed. Many in these social layers are also disillusioned regarding their vague expectations of a profound improvement in society through reformist socialism.

The reformist parties and trade-union leaders betrayed the revolution, capitulated to capitalism, and formed a coalition with the bourgeoisie in order to restore class rule and class exploitation as of old. All this they did under the banner of "democracy." As a result, this type of "sympathizer" with the proletariat has been led to doubt socialism itself and its capacity to bring liberation and renew society. The immense majority of the proletariat outside Soviet Russia tolerated this betrayal with a weak-willed fear of struggle and submitted to their own exploitation and enslavement. Among the layers in ferment among the small and middle bourgeoisie and intellectuals, this shattered any belief in the working class as a powerful agent of radical social change. They have been joined by many proletarian forces who seek and demand action and are dissatisfied with the conduct of all the political parties. In addition fascism attracted a social layer, the former officers, who lost their careers when the war ended. Now without income, they were disillusioned, uprooted, and torn from their class roots. This is especially true in the vanquished Central Powers [Germany and Austria-Hungary], in which fascism takes on a strong antirepublican flavor.

Lacking historical understanding and political education, the socially variegated and hastily assembled violent bands of fascism expect everything to be put right by a state that is their own creation and tool. Supposedly standing above class and party, this state is to carry out their confused and contradictory program in accordance with or in violation of bourgeois legality, utilizing either "democracy" or a dictator.

In the period of revolutionary ferment and upsurge by the proletariat, fascism flirted to some degree with proletarian-revolutionary demands.

The masses following fascism vacillated between the two armies expressing the overriding world-historical class antagonisms and class struggles. However, after capitalist rule was reasserted and the bourgeoisie began a general offensive, fascism came down firmly on the side of the bourgeoisie, a commitment held by their leaders from the very start.

The bourgeoisie was quick to recruit fascism to service and use in its struggle to beat down and permanently enslave the proletariat. As the dislocation of the capitalist economy extends over time and deepens, the burdens and suffering that this imposes on the proletariat become more intolerable. And so, too, the protection against the pressure of the working masses offered to the bourgeois order by reformist sermons on civil peace and democratic class collaboration grow ineffective. The bourgeoisie needs to use aggressive force to defend itself against the working class. The old and seemingly "apolitical" repressive apparatus of the bourgeois state no longer provides it with sufficient security. The bourgeoisie moves to create special bands of class struggle against the proletariat. Fascism provides such troops. Although fascism includes revolutionary currents related to its origin and the forces supporting it—currents that could turn against capitalism and its state—it nonetheless develops into a dangerous force for counterrevolution. That is clearly shown in the country where it triumphed: Italy.

Fascism clearly will display different features in each country, flowing from the given historical circumstances. But it consists everywhere of an amalgam of brutal, terrorist violence together with deceptive revolutionary phraseology, linking up demagogically with the needs and moods of broad masses of producers. It has reached its most mature expression so far in Italy. Here the passivity of the Socialist Party and the reformist trade-union leaders opened every door to it. And its revolutionary language won it the support of many proletarian forces, who made its victory possible.

The development of fascism in Italy expresses the inability of the party and unions to utilize the workers' occupation of the factories in 1920 to heighten the proletarian class struggle. The fascist victory violently obstructs every workers' movement, even for simple and nonpolitical wage demands. The fascist victory in Italy goads the bourgeoisie of other countries to have the proletariat struck down in the same fashion. The working class of the entire world is threatened with the fate of its Italian brothers.

However, the development of fascism in Italy displays something else as well. Fascism has a contradictory character and carries within it strong elements of ideological and political dislocation and dissolution. Its goal is to recast the old bourgeois "democratic" state into a fascist state based on violence. This unleashes conflicts between the old established bureaucracy and the new fascist one; between the standing army with its officer corps and the new militia with its leaders; between violent fascist policies in the economy and state and the ideology of the remaining liberal and democratic bourgeoisie; between monarchists and republicans; between the actual fascists (the blackshirts) and the nationalists recruited into the party and its militia; between the fascists' original program, which deceived the masses and achieved victory, and present-day fascist politics, which serve the interests of industrial capitalists and above all of heavy industry, which has been propped up artificially.

Underlying these and other conflicts, however, are the insurmountable and irreconcilable economic and social conflicts among the different capitalist social layers: between the big bourgeoisie and the small and middle bourgeoisie such as the small peasantry and the intelligentsia. And towering over everything is the greatest of all economic and social conflicts: the class conflict between bourgeoisie and proletariat.

The indicated conflicts have already found expression in the ideological bankruptcy of fascism, through the contradiction between the fascist program and the way it is being carried out. Resolving these conflicts may be hindered for a time by organized armed bands and unscrupulous terror. Ultimately, however, these conflicts will find expression in armed force and will tear fascism apart.

The revolutionary vanguard of the proletariat cannot look on passively as fascism disintegrates. Its historical duty, instead, lies in hastening and promoting this process consciously and actively. Fascism encompasses confused and unwittingly revolutionary forces that must be led to join the proletarian class struggle against the class rule and violent exploitation of the bourgeoisie. The military defeat of fascism must be prepared by surmounting it ideologically and politically.

The conscious revolutionary vanguard of the working class has the task of taking up the struggle against victorious fascism in Italy and the fascism now taking shape around the world. It must disarm and overcome fascism politically and must organize the workers into strong and successful self-defense against its violent actions. To this end, the following tasks are posed:

I

A special structure to lead the struggle against fascism, made up of workers' parties and organizations of every viewpoint, must be formed in every country. The tasks of this structure are:

1) Collecting facts on the fascist movement in every country.

2) Methodical education of the working class regarding the hostile class character of the fascist movement through newspaper articles, pamphlets, posters, assemblies, and so on.

3) Methodical education of the masses who have just become proletarians or are threatened by inevitable proletarianization regarding their condition and the function of fascism in assisting large-scale capitalism.

4) Organization of defensive struggles by the working class by forming and arming contingents of self-defense. Given that the fascists concentrate on propaganda among youth and that worker youth must be drawn into the united front, youth who are more than seventeen years old must be recruited into the common factory-based fighting contingents. Workers' control commissions must be organized to prevent transport of fascist bands and their

weapons. Fascist attempts to terrorize the workers and block expressions of their class activity must be mercilessly struck down.

5) Workers of all viewpoints must be drawn into this struggle. All workers' parties, trade unions, and proletarian mass organizations must be called on to join the common defense against fascism.

6) A struggle against fascism is needed in parliament and in all public institutions. Strong emphasis must be laid on the imperialist and arch-chauvinist nature of fascism, which heightens the danger of new international wars.

II

Fascist forces are organizing internationally, and the workers' struggle against fascism must also organize on a world scale. To this end, an international workers' committee needs to be created. The task of this committee is to exchange experiences and organize international actions, above all against Italian fascism and its representatives abroad. This struggle includes the following measures:

1) A campaign of international education through newspapers, pamphlets, posters, and mass meetings regarding the Italian fascist leadership's total hostility to workers and its methodical destruction of all workers' organizations and institutions.

2) Organization of international mass meetings and demonstrations against fascism and against Italian fascism's representatives abroad.

3) Struggle in parliament. Demand that parliament, the workers' fractions within it, and international workers' organizations send commissions to Italy to investigate the condition of the working class there.

4) Struggle for immediate liberation of arrested or imprisoned Communist, Socialist, or nonparty workers.

5) Organization of an international boycott by all workers against Italy. Refuse to ship coal to Italy. All transport workers must refuse to load and ship goods to and from Italy, and so on. To this end, create an international committee of miners, seamen, railway workers, and transport workers in every field.

6) Material and moral support of the persecuted working class of Italy through collections of funds, accommodation of refugees, support of their work abroad, and so on. Expand International Red Aid in order to carry out this work.[1] Involve workers' cooperatives in this assistance work.

It must be brought home to workers' attention that the fate of the Italian working class will be theirs as well, unless they block the influx of less class-conscious forces to fascism through energetic revolutionary struggle against the ruling class. Workers' organizations therefore must display great energy, in their offensive against capitalism, in protecting the broad masses of producers against exploitation, oppression, and usury. In this way they will counterpose earnest organized mass struggle to the fake revolutionary and demagogic slogans of fascism. In addition, they must strike down the first attempts to organize fascism in their own country, keeping in mind that fascism in Italy and internationally can be most successfully resisted through an energetic struggle against it in their own country.

APPENDIX A
THE FRANKFURT CONFERENCE
AGAINST FASCISM

Introductory Note

An international conference against fascism and war took place in Frankfurt am Main, Germany, on March 17–20, 1923. The conference was held in the wake of the January 1923 invasion and occupation of the Ruhr by French and Belgian troops.

The conference was initiated by the Rhine-Westphalia factory committees with a call to all labor organizations to participate; the Communist International's Executive Committee quickly accepted the invitation.

The nearly 250 delegates included representatives from Germany, France, Italy, Britain, Soviet Russia, Holland, Czechoslovakia, Poland, Austria, Bulgaria, India, and Switzerland. Envisioned as a united-front effort, the meeting was attended by representatives from a number of Communist parties, as well as by representatives from unions and other workers' organizations. Although the German Social Democratic Party (SPD) and Independent Social Democratic Party (USPD) leaderships turned down a request to participate, twenty-nine representatives from local units of these parties did so. Representatives from the Communist International's Executive Committee, the Communist Youth International, and the Red International of Labor Unions also attended.

A prominent role was played at the conference by the Provisional International Committee for Combating Fascism. Formed on the Comintern's initiative in January 1923, this committee had issued a call to the world proletariat for united action against fascism. Along these lines, it appealed to the Second International, the social democratic World Federation of Trade Unions, and syndicalist unions to join in the effort. Zetkin was chair of the Provisional Committee, and, as such, she played a central role in the Frankfurt conference, giving the main report on the struggle against fascism.

At the conclusion of the meeting, the Frankfurt conference elected an International Action Committee Against War and Fascism of twenty-one members, headed by Zetkin and French writer and Communist Henri Barbusse.

Below is the abbreviated account of Zetkin's report to the conference published at the time in the Comintern press, translated by Sean Larson, together with the resolution adopted on the struggle against fascism.

¶

Report on Fascism

The occupation of the Ruhr has fanned the flames of the fascist menace, which threatens all workers regardless of whether they are in the ranks of the meek Social Democratic organizations or the ill-reputed Communist ones. Fascism signifies the danger of the world proletariat sliding into a new world war, greater and more barbaric in its scope than all the barbarity, infamy, and crime that we experienced during the imperialist world war. But even beyond that, fascism's nationalist slogans split and paralyze the working class. In this way, it threatens to destroy the fighting international proletariat, the sole power capable of defeating not only the giants of the French mining and steel industries but also the coal and finance magnates of Germany and the whole world.

In order to bring this struggle to victory, it is necessary to clearly understand the character of fascism. Some comrades judge it too simplistically, regarding fascism as a phenomenon of white terror, an expression of the fighting strength of the bourgeoisie. Despite the superficial similarities between the Horthy terror and fascism, they are in essence different phenomena. The white terror in Hungary came as a consequence of the forceful and—it must be said—not inglorious attempt by the Hungarian proletarians to bring down capitalism through the construction of a council republic. After the revolution was crushed, a small stratum of Junkers and militarists established their tyranny in this primarily agrarian country. Fascism in the modern industrial states is completely different. It takes shape as a broad-based mass movement, composed not only of petty bourgeois and small-holding peasants, but also of unenlightened proletarian forces.

Fascism is the expression of the economic decay of capitalism and the disintegration of the bourgeois state.

How was fascism able to develop into a mass movement that won out against the workers' movement in Italy? This was possible only through the decomposition of bourgeois society. Broad swathes of the petty bourgeoisie and the intellectuals have lost their prewar conditions of life; they were not just proletarianized, they were pauperized. The bourgeois economy was incapable of securing the existence of these layers of the proletariat, dragging them instead into the lumpenproletariat. To these we can add the civil servants and employees, whose existence cannot be secured by a bankruptcy-threatened state. Once the firmest supports of the bourgeois state, they are now partly indifferent, partly hostile toward the bourgeois government. But fascist slogans are gathering support among many who previously put their faith in socialist slogans, who without any clear insight felt instinctively opposed to big capital and hoped for improvements through the taming of capitalism on the road to democracy. This hope was bitterly deceived by the reformist parties because, today, even reforms within bourgeois society can be achieved only by revolutionary class struggle. This group is joined by a number of decommissioned officers, a surplus of which was created during the war. The fascist organizations are fashioning themselves into a *refuge for the politically homeless.*

This conforms to their political program. The present state is to be replaced by a kind of neutered entity that stands above the parties and classes. The program varies not only from country to country but even within a single country. It is not only the intense ruination brought about by defeat in war, as in Germany, that prepares the ground for fascism. This is proven by the fact that fascism has triumphed in Italy. Mussolini founded his first organizations in March 1919 with an explicitly republican program, which made the finest promises to the bourgeoisie and petty bourgeoisie, to the workers and the agrarians alike. In reality only one point of the program has been retained from the first day until now: *bitter hostility to the socialist workers' organizations.*

The Italian premier Giolitti, whose beheading Mussolini was demanding in those days, could have easily tamed the movement, but he preferred to place it in the service of the bourgeoisie. The agrarian elements pouring into the fascist camp knew they had to take a hard stance regarding Mussolini's republicanism. The antagonism between agrarian capital and industrial capital, the one longing for the old social relations of bondage, the other wishing to establish a modern industrial state, continues within the party to this day. It is primarily due to the effects of the economic crisis that the fascist organizations could grow to such an extent, even though in May 1920 they mustered only 4,000 votes in their stronghold of Milan. Punitive expeditions were organized; trade union and cooperative headquarters were burned to the ground; leaders of the workers' movement were murdered. The number of fascists is now thought to be half a million, and the strength of their military units when they seized power was estimated at

300,000 men. On top of this, national corporative associations that reject the class struggle were created, economic organizations that brought together workers, employers, and mid-level employees of all stripes in a given line of work. With the class-conscious workers suppressed by bloody force and the scourge of hunger, chased out of work and driven from their homes, the fascist organizations could raise their numbers to half a million members, although they are not by any means all convinced fascists. Mussolini made the further attempt to utterly corrupt the "free" trade unions by *offering them participation in government.*

The disgraceful offer was a failure, not by any merit of the unions however, but rather because of the resistance put up by the industrial and agrarian financiers of the fascists.

All of this was possible only because the Italian Socialist Party did not understand that it needed to assemble the working masses into a resolute power steeled to fight. Instead of opposing force with force, it wanted to take on fascism with moral sermons and sweet flute-like melodies. It is a vital necessity for the proletariat of all countries to draw the lesson from the Italian example: *There can be no wavering, no backing down. We must undertake the struggle against fascism with vigor from the very first moment.*

Italian fascism is already extending its web into Germany. It has an organization in Berlin. The Hitler gangs who reign in Bavaria are already transforming it into a fascist state. How else can you explain the shameful treatment of political prisoners except as the terror of fascism? Although in Bavaria the fascist program is exhausted by the phrase "beat up the Jews," the program of the North German organizations is full of pseudo-revolutionary phrases, though without concrete measures for their implementation and all of it cloaked in the steel armor of the national ethos.

We must grapple with this national ideology explicitly. We still hold to the words "the proletarian has no fatherland," because everything that could make a fatherland into a fatherland is extracted by capitalist exploitation, up to and including the very light of the sun. In spite of this, the proletariat is connected to the material and cultural wealth which is the product of many generations, and which it alone can transfer to coming generations. That is why the proletariat will create its fatherland through its own efforts, by constructing its government and constituting itself as a nation.

It is time to draw the practical conclusions. In every country, committees made up of proletarians of all parties must be organized for systematic struggle against fascism. But the first rule must be: *self-defense of the workers, in order to confront force with force.*

We must take on the organization of the self-defense groups in the factories, of control committees to supervise and prevent the transport of weapons and troops. The arming of the workers is important not only for the fight against fascism, but also for the conflict with capitalism as a whole. The clamor of the bourgeois press demonstrates that they understand this well: *Weapons in the hands of the working class mean the disarming, the overpowering of the bourgeoisie.*

In order to combat fascism internationally, above all the fascist government in Italy, we need an *international action committee*. It must gather material and conduct propaganda and, beyond that, take up the fight for the immediate release of all revolutionary fighters thrown in jail by the fascists. In recent weeks approximately 8,000 workers were put behind prison walls. Here too the international committee must complete the work prepared by the national committees, namely *the boycott of fascist Italy.*

Most important will be preventing imports from Britain and the United States, without which Italy cannot go on. The most effective way to fight fascism in Italy, however, is and remains fighting fascism in every individual country. To this end, workers everywhere must join forces to enter into battle. In Russia, the proletariat has emerged from all the horrors of the white terror, having defeated all of its enemies. This they could do because they possessed the faith that can move mountains, the faith in their own power. The German proletarians too must hold firmly to this faith. Only then will it find the strength to fight and to win. (*Enthusiastic applause*)

Summary remarks

The relative stability of the bourgeois state in France flows from the low level of development of French capitalism, which has not yet brought the class antagonisms to their extremes. The imperialist ascendancy of France in Europe would change that. The conference cannot entirely agree with the suggestions of the Italian comrade [Combiancchi]. We must not replace Marxism with the biblical principle, "An eye for an eye, a tooth for a tooth."

Individual terror is unable to bring the self-confidence of the proletariat to fruition. Our most effective weapon is organized mass
struggle. Not only must we put down fascism with force, we also
have to vanquish it politically. Let us go forward in our struggle
against the general offensive of capital, against the fascist terror,
for the construction of a workers' government and, beyond that,
the dictatorship of the proletariat, which alone can provide the
guarantee that the proletariat will be rid of every form of counterrevolution.[1] (*Loud applause*)

§

Resolution on the Struggle Against Fascism

An additional task is imposed on the working class, that of fighting victorious fascism in Italy, and fascism being organized all
over the world. It must overcome fascism politically and organize
effective means of self-defense against fascist violence. For this
purpose, the following measures must be adopted:

1. Labor parties and labor organizations of every tendency
   must form a special body in each country for leading
   the struggle against fascism. The duties of such a body
   are as follows:

   (a) Compilation of facts on the fascist movement in
   their own countries.

(b) Systematic education of the working class as to the hostile class character of the fascist movement, by means of newspaper articles, pamphlets, posters, meetings, etc.

(c) Organization of self-defense among the working class by means of enrolling and arming self-defense troops. Organization of workers' control committees to prevent the transport of fascist bands and their weapons. Ruthless suppression of all fascist attempts to terrorize the workers and hinder the expression of their class will.

(d) Inclusion of all workers, of whatever party, in this struggle. Appeal to all labor parties, trade unions, and all proletarian mass organizations, to join in defense against fascism.

(e) Combat fascism in parliaments and all public bodies.

(f) Special attention to antifascist education among working youth, from whose ranks the fascists enlist most of their recruits. The revolutionary youth organizations should take part in the activity of all the proletarian organizations of self-defense.

2. The forces of fascism are organized internationally. It is therefore imperative that the fight against fascism also be organized internationally. For this purpose, an international workers' committee must be formed. In addition to serving as a vehicle for exchanging experiences, this committee will above all be entrusted with the organization of the international struggle, to be conducted chiefly against

Italian fascism. Leading elements in this struggle are:

(a) An international campaign of enlightenment by means of newspapers, pamphlets, pictures, mass meetings, etc., showing the absolutely anti-working-class character of Italian fascist rule, and the systematic destruction of all labor organizations and institutions by fascism.

(b) The organization of international mass meetings and demonstrations against fascism, against the representatives of the Italian fascist state abroad, etc.

(c) Utilization of parliaments; appeals to parliaments, especially to their labor fractions, and to international labor organizations, to send commissions to Italy to examine the situation of the working class.

(d) Struggle for the immediate liberation of all imprisoned revolutionary proletarian fighters.

3. Material and moral support for the persecuted working class of Italy by collecting money, finding homes for refugees, aiding their work abroad, etc. International Red Aid must be further developed to this end. The workers' cooperatives should be appealed to for help.

(a) The international committee of action is commissioned to consider all possibilities of a moral, political, and material boycott of the fascist government.

(b) The conference commissions the international committee of action to put itself into communication with the "Provisional International Committee for Combating Fascism," and with the organizations formed by it, for the purpose of establishing a permanent committee.

It is imperative to hammer into the minds of workers that the fate of the Italian working class will be their own fate, if they do not undertake energetic revolutionary struggle against the ruling class in order to prevent the less-class-conscious elements from being recruited to fascism. Labor organizations must therefore advance against capital with the utmost energy, for the protection of the broad masses of working people against exploitation, oppression, and extortion. They must oppose the pseudo-revolutionary demagogic watchwords of fascism with an efficiently organized mass struggle. Further, they must crush with all their might the first attempts at fascist organization in their own countries.

APPENDIX B
ZETKIN'S APPEAL
FOR A UNITED FRONT
AGAINST NAZISM

John Riddell

Twelve months after the adoption of Clara Zetkin's report and resolution on fascism, this position was overturned by the Comintern's Fifth World Congress, held in June–July 1924.

During the next few years, as the International came increasingly under the domination of a bureaucratic apparatus headed by Joseph Stalin, its view on fascism and the united front shifted several times, without ever returning fully to its 1923 position. Then in 1928 the Comintern embraced a sectarian stance, opposed in principle to antifascist unity of any kind with Social Democratic and other non-Communist currents in the workers' movement, whom it labeled "social fascists." This refusal, combined with a corresponding rejection of united action by leaders of the Social Democratic Party (SPD), opened the door to Hitler's assumption of power in Germany in January 1933.

Although increasingly burdened by illness and loss of vision, Zetkin remained an active member of the Comintern during these years. The International's officials blocked her from openly expressing her views on fascism and the united front. Nonetheless, she found ways to indicate her disagreement on these questions. In August 1932 she managed to express the essence of her 1923 report on fascism in a speech to the German Reichstag (parliament). By the time Zetkin died a year later at the age of 75, she was one of the few leading figures within the Communist International who was still attempting to stand on the ground of the Comintern under Lenin.

About-face on workers' unity

In his opening report to the Fifth Comintern Congress in 1924, its president, Gregory Zinoviev, abandoned Zetkin's analysis of the nature and dynamics of fascism by claiming that Social Democracy was itself closely linked to this antiworker movement. "The Social Democratic Party has become a wing of fascism," he declared. "The fascists are the right hand and the Social Democrats the left hand of the bourgeoisie."[1] This ultraleft position excluded the possibility of united action involving both Communist and Social Democratic workers—the very error that had crippled resistance to Italian fascism during its rise to power in 1921–22.

Zinoviev also criticized attempts by Communist parties to promote the cause of workers' unity in action by challenging and, when appropriate, negotiating with Social Democrats on a leadership level—an approach that had been endorsed by the Fourth Comintern Congress in 1922 as a necessary component of united-front policy. He also redefined the Comintern's call for a workers' and peasants' government in such a way as to rule out any possibility of a governmental coalition with Social Democrats.

Despite opposition by Zetkin and Karl Radek, another central Comintern leader, Zinoviev's views were adopted by the 1924 Congress.

Rise of Stalinism

The underlying cause of the turnabout in Comintern policy was the rise of a privileged and self-serving bureaucratic layer within the Russian Communist Party and a resulting factional division in its leadership. In 1923, a Left Opposition led by Leon Trotsky and supported by Radek renewed the antibureaucratic struggle launched by Lenin in 1922.[2] Lenin's political activity had been cut short by a stroke in March 1923; he died in January 1924. While Lenin was incapacitated, Zinoviev was part of a bloc with Lev Kamenev and Joseph Stalin to take over the Communist Party's leadership and to oppose Trotsky. By the end of 1923, Trotsky and Radek had been thrust aside from their central leadership role in the Comintern.[3]

Zinoviev, who had initially held doubts about the united-front policy,[4] threw his authority in 1924 behind an ultraleft shift, particularly with regard to Germany. With Lenin gone and Trotsky and Radek sidelined, Zetkin was left as the only leading proponent of united-front policy in the broader Comintern leadership.

The debate at the Communist International's Fifth Congress focused on drawing a balance sheet of the German Communist Party (KPD)'s participation in the massive workers' upsurge in Germany in 1923, which the Comintern central leadership believed could have led to a successful proletarian revolution. After months of intense struggle in Germany, capitalist rule was restabilized by year-end, with the Communist Party in inglorious retreat. Debate over the causes of this defeat spread to the Russian party. Trotsky and the Left Opposition accused the Comintern Executive (ECCI) of failing to see the revolutionary potential of the situation until it was too late. Zinoviev sought to pin responsibility on the German party's main leaders, Heinrich Brandler and August Thalheimer, who like Zetkin were strong advocates of broad united action against fascism.

In 1924 the ECCI under Zinoviev threw its support behind the ultraleft current in Germany led by Ruth Fischer and endorsed its retreat from united-front initiatives. Meanwhile, the Comintern Executive forced all its parties into alignment with the Zinoviev-Kamenev-Stalin "troika" in the Russian party. Zetkin kept silent on the Russian dispute, refusing to endorse the "troika," but she did speak up on the united-front debate in Germany.

Zetkin at the Fifth Congress

Both Zetkin and Radek took the floor at the Fifth Congress to strongly oppose Zinoviev's proposals to reverse Comintern positions on the united front and other questions. Most of Zetkin's two-hour speech was devoted to the defeat in Germany. While making forceful criticisms of the German party's leadership, she also pointed to the ECCI's responsibility and argued that the German working class had not been ready in the autumn of 1923 for a showdown struggle for power.

The last half-hour of Zetkin's speech dealt with the united front, the underlying issue behind the disagreement on fascism. The basic precondition for united-front efforts, she explained, was the Communist Party's unity, independence, and close ties to the masses. In that framework, negotiations with Social Democratic leaders were sometimes appropriate—provided that we meet with them "not to do them honor" but to "increase the pressure on them toward action" and win "an even broader range of their supporters to our banner." Delegates should not reject such leadership meetings on principle, she said. They should hold firm to the decisions of the Fourth Congress (1922) on this point and not be misled by latter-day reinterpretations of them.[5] Despite Zetkin's appeal, the Fifth Congress endorsed Zinoviev's proposals.

Although sharply criticized at the congress, Zetkin was still publicly honored by the Comintern in the years that followed as a symbol of revolutionary intransigence. She often penned greetings or appeals of a ceremonial nature, but was not allowed to speak or write publicly on controversial topics. The journal *Die*

Kommunistische Fraueninternationale (The Communist Women's International), in which she was the driving force, was shut down in 1925.

Zetkin was severely afflicted by illness during the last decade of her life. Her lengthy periods of treatment outside Moscow sometimes served, according to her biographer Tânia Puschnerat, as a form of quarantine to keep her away from important political occasions.[6]

Defending unity in struggle

Zinoviev broke with Stalin in 1925 and went into opposition, joining the next year with Trotsky, Kamenev, and Radek in the United Opposition, which challenged the tightening grip of Stalin's bureaucratic control in the Soviet Union and his rejection of an internationalist perspective under the guise of building "socialism in one country." The Ruth Fischer leadership in the German party (KPD), aligned with Zinoviev, was overturned at the end of 1926. During the interval that followed, Zetkin regained limited freedom of action within the Comintern leadership. In 1927 she became once more a member of the KPD Central Committee; she was removed two years later.

In October 1927, Zetkin sent the KPD Central Committee a powerful defense of the united-front policies she had helped develop in 1921–23. She called on the party to propose conditional support to a Social Democratic government in the German federal state of Hamburg, where the KPD and SPD together held a parliamentary majority, on the basis of an agreed program of measures in workers' interests. Zetkin's letter also defended the KPD's entry in 1923 into a short-lived SPD-KPD government in the German state of Saxony, which had been sharply attacked within the KPD and the International.

"We can be sure that the broad masses have a quite incorrect view of what such a government could achieve," she wrote, "but this is all the more reason to call for it." Otherwise, she believed, the SPD leaders would find it all the easier to reject governing with KPD support and to form a coalition instead with the openly bourgeois parties—its standard procedure during the years of Germany's 1919–33 Weimar Republic.[7]

At this time, Zetkin was aligned with Nikolai Bukharin, then the Comintern's president. Zetkin supported Bukharin and Stalin's harsh reprisals against the United Opposition, going so far as to endorse Trotsky's expulsion from the Communist Party in November 1927. She did not protest the mass arrests of oppositionists and their banishment to Siberia. She thereby gave encouragement to bureaucratic forces that were soon to turn against Bukharin and solidify Stalin's absolute rule.[8]

Ultraleft turn

Only one month after Zetkin's appeal on the united front, a convention of the Communist Party of the Soviet Union initiated a major ultraleft turn in policy. Known as the "Third Period" line, it was based on a schema according to which the first period was the revolutionary upsurge that followed World War I; the second period was the stabilization of capitalism that followed; the third period was supposedly to be marked by capitalist collapse and revolution. It served to solidify Stalin's control by undercutting support for Bukharin as well as to win over and silence individuals sympathetic to Trotsky and the Left Opposition. The new line began the march toward forced collectivization of agriculture, breakneck industrialization, and ever-tightening control by the Stalinist bureaucracy in the Soviet Union.

In Germany, this line meant reviving and intensifying the disastrous policies of the Ruth Fischer period, including rejection of united-front initiatives with the Social Democrats. Stalin made a rare appearance at an ECCI meeting in February 1928 to castigate the "right wing" of the KPD—that is, the forces led by Brandler and associated with Zetkin—as the main danger to the party. The meeting marked the effective end of united-front policy in the Comintern, blocking the road to a fighting antifascist alliance. A subsequent meeting of delegates from Germany and the Soviet Union to the ECCI, from which Zetkin was excluded, spelled out the transfer of power in the KPD to forces adhering to Stalin's new line.

Zetkin expressed her anguish in a letter to her son Costia in March 1928: "I ask myself, what to do. . . . This situation afflicts and torments me." She wrote German party leader Wilhelm Pieck of her opposition to having such vital questions of party policy "settled by agreements among different parties," alluding to the Soviet party's interference in the KPD's internal life.[9]

When the resolution on Germany came up in the ECCI for ratification the next month, Zetkin alone voted to reject it. She wrote a confidential letter to the KPD leadership explaining her views, which was inexplicably leaked and published the following year in a German non-Communist newspaper.[10]

In the months that followed, a behind-the-scenes factional struggle opened up in the leadership of the Russian party, known since 1925 as the "All-Union Communist Party" (Bolsheviks). Stalin's faction, committed to an ultraleft line both internationally and in the Soviet Union, confronted "right oppositionist" forces led by Bukharin.

On July 3, 1929, the Moscow daily *Pravda* published an article by Zetkin that presented some central themes of her 1923 report on fascism. She submitted the article as a criticism of the draft program prepared for the Comintern congress the following month, whose main author was Bukharin. Criticizing the draft's schematic presentation of a "class against class" perspective, Zetkin stressed that the Comintern must unite "all working people and all oppressed classes and peoples." She regretted the draft program's inadequate attention to middle layers between the proletariat and bourgeoisie, especially the more educated layers ("intellectuals"). Also neglected, Zetkin indicated, was the impact of capitalist "rationalization"—increasing mechanization and the displacement of small-scale producers and traders—which was throwing all subordinate social layers into crisis. Demands benefiting women were absent, she pointed out, while the significance of women for the class struggle was acknowledged only for those who were workers or peasants. A German text of Zetkin's article circulated to Comintern activists internationally.[11]

The Comintern's Sixth Congress, held in July–August 1928,

was the first one attended by Zetkin where she did not speak. In its corridors, Stalin's supporters campaigned against Bukharin and his international supporters, including Zetkin.

The conflict in the KPD culminated in a historic session of the ECCI on December 19, 1928, where Zetkin confronted Stalin directly. Stalin's forces demanded expulsion of the KPD "right wing"; Zetkin called for postponement of any disciplinary action until the KPD held a democratic discussion and congress. During this session, Béla Kun, an architect of the ultraleft "March Action" disaster in Germany in 1921, charged Zetkin with "rightism" for opposing his course at that time. In response, Zetkin pointed out that she had joined with Lenin in rallying the world congress against Kun's ultraleft views. To no avail: the plenum decisions were in step with Kun's position. Expulsion of the KPD "right" was decided, against the votes of Zetkin, Jules Humbert-Droz, and Angelo Tasca; 6,000 dissidents were forced out of the German party.[12]

Stalin's open break with Bukharin followed several months later. Bukharin's faction was crushed; Bukharin and other leading "right oppositionists" capitulated, admitting their supposed errors. Expelled supporters of Bukharin in Germany organized a new movement, which took the name Communist Party of Germany (Opposition), or KPD(O).

Privately, Zetkin wrote bitterly of the Comintern's transformation into a mechanism that "sucks in Russian-language directives on one side and shoots them out, translated into various languages, on the other."[13] Yet she still believed that Communists must work to reform the International, as did her friends in the KPD(O) and also the now-exiled Leon Trotsky and his comrades in the International Left Opposition. For Zetkin, loyalty to this perspective and to the Soviet Union demanded that she remain in the International, even at the cost of keeping silent on crucial issues. Stalin, for his part, although threatened by Zetkin's continued defiance, evidently considered the risks flowing from her membership less than those that might follow if she were expelled.

Between October 1929 and March 1930, Zetkin composed a comprehensive memorandum on the crisis in the KPD addressed to the ECCI.[14] Assessing the German party's erroneous political line, she diagnosed it as a symptom of a more general crisis of the Comintern as a whole. As in the December 1928 ECCI plenum, she compared the party's ultraleft stance with the notorious "theory of the offensive" that some central ECCI leaders had briefly and disastrously embraced in 1921.[15] Breaking the grip of that error had been the great achievement of the Comintern's Third Congress (1921). Won through the efforts of Lenin, Trotsky, and Zetkin herself, this victory opened the door to the united-front policy adopted by the Comintern later that year.

Zetkin's memorandum condemned the destructive role of the Soviet party, which, she said, no longer "leads" but merely "dictates" to the International. And for the first and only time, she challenged the Stalin leadership's policies within the Soviet Union by demanding "extensive documentary material" on developments in the Soviet party and state. Comintern member parties, she said, had the "duty and right to consult on the problems of the Soviet Union in fraternal solidarity with the Russian party."

Expressions of dissent

Zetkin complained to her son Maxim of the severe censorship and frequent suppression of her writings. Even her name could no longer be mentioned, she said. And yet, by one means or another, her ideas managed to reach a wider audience.

In 1929, after many delays, her *Reminiscences of Lenin* was published in German. This pamphlet contained a detailed account of her collaboration with Lenin in the Third Congress over issues fundamental to united-front policy.[16]

Zetkin received visits from leaders of the KPD(O) such as Paul Frölich, with whom she agreed on the united front, trade-union unity, the need for internal party democracy, and the need to reform the Comintern. The KPD(O) published four of Zetkin's private oppositional statements, without eliciting any protest from her.[17] She corresponded with old friends now hostile to the KPD, such as Georg Ledebour. She wrote an obituary of Margarete Wengels, a comrade from wartime revolutionary struggles who later returned to the SPD, which was published in a non-KPD workers' paper.[18]

While praising the Soviet Union's achievements, Zetkin did not join in the customary adulation of the Soviet dictator.[19] She expressed her contempt for the Soviet ruler in a private note intended for Bukharin in Moscow, advising him not to let himself be pushed around by Stalin, whom she referred to, using the gendered language of that era, as a "mentally deranged woman who wears men's pants."[20]

In 1929, the Russian émigré and SPD press published rumors regarding Zetkin's supposed persecution by Communist authorities in Moscow. The KPD's central newspaper, *Die Rote Fahne,* twice broke its silence regarding Zetkin by publishing her denials of these reports. Her second statement ended in a fashion surely disconcerting to her editors: "As is generally known, my outlook on both tactics and fundamentals stands opposed to the opinion of the ECCI's majority."[21]

Although aware of the Comintern's degeneration, Zetkin maneuvered cautiously and skillfully to maintain her status as a tolerated dissident. In her 1929–30 memorandum, she pledged, "I will break party discipline three times, four times, if it serves the interests of revolution." But when, in 1931, Stalin assailed the memory of Rosa Luxemburg, for example, Zetkin's protests of this insult to her longtime friend and comrade circulated only in private letters.[22]

"My greatest affliction," she told a friend at the time, "is to answer the question: Where does the truth lie? What are my responsibilities to the proletarian revolution? Should I speak out or remain silent?" She paid the price of maintaining her Communist Party membership, which was to speak only a fraction of what she believed.[23]

Seizing an opportunity

Zetkin continued to present aspects of her 1923 analysis of fascism publicly when possible—in a criticism of KPD policy sent to party leader Wilhelm Pieck in March 1932, for example, and in published greetings to an antifascist conference in June.[24] In greeting the KPD's 1931 campaign for freedom of choice on abortion, she made a public appeal for unity with women in the SPD.[25]

In August 1932, Zetkin seized a chance to speak publicly to a national audience on the need for united action against fascism. To do so she had to leave some things unsaid, such as the need to approach the SPD to develop a united struggle against fascism. Passages from her text stressing the magnitude of the task the party faced in rousing the masses were deleted from her final text. Nonetheless, confident that she could express the essence of her thinking, she eagerly grasped the opportunity.

The circumstances of the speech were dramatic.

The global depression that broke out in 1929 had hit Germany hard. With its workers' parties consumed by fratricidal struggle, Hitler's National Socialists—in eclipse since 1923—quickly grew to be Germany's largest party. The Nazi vote rose from 2.6 percent (1928) to 18.3 percent (1930) and 37.4 percent (1932). In the July 1932 vote, Zetkin was reelected to the Reichstag, having been a member since 1920. Seventy-four years old, she was the oldest member of Germany's parliament and as such had the right to formally open its first session.

The Nazi press bristled with vile threats against her as a "Communist Jew," a "slut" (Goebbels), and a "traitor." The KPD received a Nazi threat to assault her on the floor of the Reichstag. But when her party's Central Committee asked whether she could open the Reichstag session, she responded with characteristic defiance, "I'll get there, dead or alive." Driven incognito into Berlin, she slipped into a safe house. Her biographer Gilbert

Badia describes the ensuing drama at the Reichstag as follows:

"Clara Zetkin was very weak, subject to fainting fits, and almost blind. On August 30, before a Reichstag crammed with Nazi deputies in SA and SS uniforms, two Communist deputies helped the old woman to mount the speakers' platform. She spoke at first with a barely audible voice, but little by little her voice strengthened and grew passionate."[26]

The final part of her talk reasserted the essence of her long-suppressed opinion on the urgency to forge unity against fascism.

Zetkin's Reichstag speech on fascism, 1932 (excerpts)

Our most urgent task today is to form a united front of all working people in order to turn back fascism. All the differences that divide and shackle us—whether founded on political, trade-union, religious, or ideological outlooks—must give way before this imperious historical necessity.

All those who are menaced, all those who suffer, all those who desire freedom must join the united front against fascism and its representatives in government. Working people must assert themselves against fascism. That is the urgent and indispensable precondition for a united front against economic crisis, imperialist war and its causes, and the capitalist mode of production.

The revolt of millions of laboring men and women in Germany against hunger, deprivation, fascist murder, and imperialist war expresses the imperishable destiny of producers the world over. This destiny, shared among us around the world, must find expression through forging an iron-like community of struggle of all working people in every sphere ruled by capitalism. It must also unite them with their vanguard, the liberated brothers and sisters in the Soviet Union. Strikes and uprisings in various countries abroad are blazing fires showing those who struggle in Germany that they are not alone. Everywhere the disinherited and the defeated are beginning to advance toward taking power.

Millions of women in Germany are still subjected to the chains of sexual slavery and thereby also to the most oppressive form of class slavery. They must not be absent from the united front of working people now taking shape in Germany.

The youth who want to blossom and mature must fight in the very front ranks. Today they face only the prospect of corpse-like military obedience and exploitation in the ranks of obligatory labor service.

All those who produce through intellectual labor, whose skill and will augment social well-being and culture but can find no expression in the existing bourgeois order—they too belong in the united front.

The united front must embrace all those who are dependent on wages or salaries or otherwise must pay tribute to capitalism, for it is they who both sustain capitalism and are its victims.

I am opening this session of the Reichstag in fulfillment of my duty as honorary chair and in the hope that despite my present infirmities I may yet have the good fortune to open, as honorary chair, the first congress of workers' councils of a Soviet Germany.[27]

GLOSSARY

Baldesi, Gino (1879–1934)—assistant secretary of Italian CGL union federation 1918; a leader of reformist wing of Socialist Party (PSI) and trade unions 1920–21; left PSI with reformist forces October 1922, becoming member of Unitary Socialist Party (PSU); vainly sought accommodation between CGL unions and fascists; withdrew from political activity 1927.

Barbusse, Henri (1873–1935)—French novelist; wrote about experiences in French army during World War I; joined CP 1923; a leader of International Action Committee formed by March 1923 Frankfurt conference against war and fascism.

Bauer, Otto (1881–1938)—leader and theoretician of Austrian Social Democracy; secretary of its parliamentary fraction 1907–14; prisoner of war in Russia 1914–17; Austrian minister of foreign affairs 1918–19; opponent of October Revolution and Comintern; leader of Two-and-a-Half International 1921–23; member of Bureau and Executive of Labor and Socialist International from 1923; forced into exile 1934.

Brandler, Heinrich (1881–1967)—joined SPD 1902; central figure in Chemnitz labor movement from 1914; early member of Spartacus League; a founder of German CP; convicted central leader of CP 1921–23; made scapegoat for defeat of German workers in 1923; expelled as "rightist" 1929; led Communist Party (Opposition) [KPD(O)] 1929–33; in exile 1933–49; active in Arbeiterpolitik, successor group of KPD(O), from 1949.

Bukharin, Nikolai (1888–1938)—joined Russian Bolsheviks 1906; in exile 1911–17; member Bolshevik Central Committee 1917–30; one of central leaders within Comintern from 1919; chairman of Comintern 1926–29; opposed Stalinist forced collectivization and led Right Opposition in Soviet CP 1928; deprived of leadership posts 1929; capitulated to Stalin and renounced his views; executed after Stalin frame-up trial 1938.

D'Aragona, Ludovico (1876–1961)—joined PSI 1892; a founder of Italian metalworkers' union; general secretary of CGL union federation 1918–25; SP parliamentary deputy 1919–24; opposed founding CP 1921 and remained in SP; joined reformist Unitary Socialist Party (PSU) 1922; government minister 1946–51.

Ebert, Friedrich (1871–1925)—joined SPD 1889; member of party executive committee 1905–19; succeeded Bebel as party cochairman 1913; supported German war effort in World War I; as leader of provisional government coming out of 1918 revolution, he joined with monarchists to defeat workers' uprisings 1919–20; German president 1919–25.

Fischer, Ruth (1895–1961)—cofounder of Austrian CP 1918; moved to Berlin 1919; leader of leftist opposition in German CP; gained central party leadership 1924; ECCI intervention led to her removal from German CP leadership 1925; supported United Opposition led by Trotsky and Zinoviev in Soviet CP 1926; expelled from German CP 1926; co-founder of Leninbund 1928; collaborated with Trotsky 1933–36; in exile in France and United States from 1933.

Frölich, Paul (1884–1953)—joined SPD 1902; worked as journalist for party papers in Leipzig, Hamburg, and Bremen; a supporter of Zimmerwald Left during World War I; led International Communists of Germany (IKD), which became part of CP at 1918 founding congress; participant in Bavarian Soviet Republic 1919; member of Central Committee 1919–23; expelled from CP 1928, joining Communist Party (Opposition) and later Socialist Workers' Party (SAP).

Giolitti, Giovanni (1842–1928)—Italian prime minister five times during 1892–1921; tolerated violent attacks by fascist bands 1921 and initially supported fascist regime 1922–24.

Groener, Wilhelm (1867–1939)—German general during World War I; helped suppress revolutionary workers during 1918–19 revolution; minister of transport (1920–23), defense (1928–32), and interior (1931–32).

Hitler, Adolf (1889–1945)—became leader of National Socialist Workers [Nazi] Party 1921; became chancellor January 1933; German dictator until his death.

Horthy, Miklós (1868–1957)—Austro-Hungarian naval commander during World War I; a leader of counterrevolutionary forces that crushed Hungarian soviet republic 1919 and carried out white terror; regent and dictator of Hungary 1920–44.

Humbert-Droz, Jules (1891–1971)—joined Swiss SDP 1911; internationalist during World War I; founding member CP 1921; elected to ECCI 1921; aligned with Bukharin in late 1920s; removed from Comintern posts 1928; in disfavor with Stalin leadership until 1935; leader of Swiss CP 1935–41; expelled 1943; joined SDP and became its secretary 1947–58; leader of dissident SP from 1959; in final years, supporter of Algerian freedom struggle and antiwar activist.

Kamenev, Lev (1883–1936)—joined Russian Social Democratic Party 1901; became Bolshevik 1903; arrested and exiled to Siberia 1914–17; in Petrograd 1917; elected to Central Committee 1917; elected president of Moscow Soviet 1918; member of RCP politburo; allied with Stalin and Zinoviev against Trotsky 1923–25; member of joint opposition with Trotsky 1926–27; expelled 1927; recanted and reinstated 1928; expelled again 1932; condemned to death and executed following first Moscow Trial.

Ledebour, Georg (1850–1947)—joined SPD 1891; Reichstag member 1900–18; in SPD's left wing before 1914; opposed social chauvinism during World War I; co-chair of USPD 1917–19; opposed affiliation to Comintern 1920 and remained in rump USPD; refused to rejoin SPD in 1922 fusion; led Socialist League during 1920s; member of Socialist Workers Party (SAP) 1931; fled to Switzerland 1933; continued anti-Nazi and socialist activity until his death.

Liebknecht, Karl (1871–1919)—joined German SPD 1900; first president of Socialist Youth International 1907–10; first member of German Reichstag to vote against war credits December 1914; a founder of Spartacus current; imprisoned for antiwar propaganda 1916; freed by 1918 revolution; a founding leader of German CP December 1918; murdered by rightist officers during Berlin workers' uprising January 1919.

Luxemburg, Rosa (1871–1919)—born in Poland; a founder of Polish Social Democratic SDKPiL 1893; later lived in Germany; led SPD left wing in opposition to revisionist right wing and, after 1910, against "Marxist Center" led by Kautsky; leader of Spartacus current during World War I; imprisoned 1916–18; founding leader of German CP December 1918; arrested and murdered during workers' uprising in Berlin January 1919.

Mussolini, Benito (1883–1945)—former leader of Italian SP left wing and editor of *Avanti;* took chauvinist, prowar position and was expelled from PSI 1915; founded fascist movement 1919; dictator of Italy 1922–43; executed by resistance forces.

PSI (Italian Socialist Party)—founded 1892; participated in Zimmerwald movement during World War I; affiliated to Comintern 1919; refused to expel reformist right wing; left wing split off at January 1921 Livorno congress to form CP; 200,000 members before Livorno congress, dropping to 112,000 by October 1921 and 65,000 a year later; expelled Turati and right wing 1922; 32,000 members October 1922; pro-Comintern minority joined CP 1924.

Radek, Karl (1885–1939)—joined revolutionary movement in Austrian Poland before 1905; a leader of left wing of Polish and German workers' movement; collaborator of Lenin and supporter of Zimmerwald Left during World War I; joined Bolsheviks 1917; member of Bolshevik Central Committee 1917–24; Bolshevik and Soviet emissary to Germany 1918–19; member ECCI 1920–24 and its Presidium 1921–24; with Trotsky, a leader of Left Opposition in Russian CP and Comintern from 1923; expelled and exiled 1927; capitulated to Stalin 1929; prominent Soviet journalist 1930–36; arrested 1936; convicted in Moscow trial 1937; killed by police agent in prison.

Second International—founded 1889 as international association of workers' parties; collapsed at outbreak of World War I; pro-capitalist right wing reconstituted as Bern International 1919; merged with centrist Two-and-a-Half International 1923 and became Labor and Socialist International.

Stalin, Joseph (1879–1953)—joined RSDLP 1898; Bolshevik from 1903; Central Committee member 1912; people's commissar of nationalities after October Revolution; became general secretary of Russian CP 1922; presided over degeneration of CP and Comintern; organized purges in 1930s that liquidated majority of Bolshevik leading cadre.

Stinnes, Hugo (1870–1924)—German industrialist; built vast economic empire after World War I, starting from coal and steel industry, moving to media, public utilities, banks, and other areas; during 1918 revolution, negotiated concessions to trade unions; later campaigned against eight-hour day and nationalization; had ties to far-right; opposed Versailles Treaty.

Tasca, Angelo (1892–1960)—joined Italian SP youth 1909; a founder of CP 1921; favored united action with SP; member ECCI 1924; arrested by fascists 1923, 1926; emigrated to France 1927; expelled from CP for anti-Stalinist positions 1929; rejoined PSI 1935; after 1945, wrote works of political history.

Thalheimer, August (1884–1948)—joined SPD 1904; member of Spartacus group during World War I; played prominent role in 1918 revolution in Stuttgart; member of Central Committee of German CP 1919–24; held responsible, with Brandler, for workers' defeat in October 1923; taught philosophy in Moscow 1924–28; opposed Stalin's ultraleft course 1928; expelled as "rightist" 1929; cofounder with Brandler of KPD(O); emigrated 1933; Allied powers refused his re-entry into Germany after 1945; died in Cuba.

Trotsky, Leon (1879–1940)—born in Ukraine; joined socialist movement 1897; supported Mensheviks at RSDLP congress 1903; internationalist and supporter of Zimmerwald movement during World War I; joined Bolsheviks and elected to Central Committee 1917; people's commissar of foreign affairs 1917–18 and of war 1918–25; leader of Left Opposition in Russian CP and Comintern from 1923; expelled 1927; exiled abroad 1929; called for new International 1933; main target of 1936–38 Stalin frame-up trials; founding leader of Fourth International 1938; murdered by agent of Stalin.

Turati, Filippo (1857–1932)—founding member Italian SP 1892; leader of its reformist right wing; parliamentary deputy 1896–1926; opposed Italy's entry into World War I but supported national defense as war went on; opponent of October Revolution and Comintern; expelled from PSI 1922, forming reformist PSU; emigrated to France 1926.

Two-and-a-Half International—term used by Communists for the International Working Union of Socialist Parties, or Vienna Union, an alliance of centrist social-democratic parties formed February 1921; merged with Second International to become Labor and Socialist International 1923.

USPD (Independent Social Democratic Party of Germany)—formed 1917 by left critics of SPD majority leadership; 800,000 members by end of 1920; majority fused with CP December 1920; minority retained name until merger with SPD November 1922; 210,000 members at time of merger.

Versailles Treaty—peace treaty signed June 28, 1919 between Allied powers and Germany. Among its provisions, the Treaty transferred 10 percent of Germany's territory to France, Belgium, Denmark, and Poland, and established that Germany would pay $33 billion ($461 billion in 2016 dollars) in reparations to the Entente powers. It also restricted Germany's military and provided for occupation of German territory west of the Rhine by Entente armies for fifteen years, beginning in 1920.

Wengels, Margarete (1856–1931)—joined SPD during 1870s; active in Berlin underground during Anti-Socialist Laws; a leader of socialist women's movement in Germany, collaborating closely with Zetkin; a member of USPD after 1917, she remained in that centrist party after KPD was formed; a member of SPD from 1922.

Zetkin, Clara (1857–1933)—joined German socialist movement 1878; driven into exile by Bismarck's Anti-Socialist Laws 1882–90; cofounder of Second International 1889; a leader of its Marxist wing; campaigner for women's emancipation; editor of SPD's newspaper directed to women, *Die Gleichheit*, 1891–1917; close associate of Rosa Luxemburg in SPD left wing; organized internationalist conference of socialist women 1915; joined German CP 1919; opposed ultraleftism in CP during March Action 1921 and thereafter; member ECCI from 1922; headed Communist Women's Movement 1921–26; opposed "bolshevization" campaign 1924–25 and Stalin's ultraleft turn from 1928; remained prominent figure in German CP and Comintern, without recanting, until her death in Moscow.

Zinoviev, Gregory (1883–1936)—joined Russian Social Democratic Party 1901; Bolshevik; elected to Central Committee 1907; internationalist and collaborator of Lenin during World War I; chair of Petrograd soviet 1917–26; chairman of Comintern 1919–26; on death of Lenin, collaborated with Stalin to isolate Trotsky from central leadership 1923–24; broke with Stalin 1925; with Trotsky, led United Opposition to bureaucratic degeneration 1926–27; expelled 1927; recanted and was readmitted 1928; re-expelled 1932 and 1934; convicted in Moscow frame-up trial and shot.

WORKS CITED

Badia, Gilbert. *Clara Zetkin, féministe sans frontières*. Paris: Éditions Ouvrières, 1993.

Comintern. *Protokoll Fünfter Kongress der Kommunistischen Internationale*. Hamburg: Carl Hoym Nachf., 1924.

————. *VII Congress of the Communist International: Abridged Stenographic Report of Proceedings*. Moscow: Foreign Languages Publishing House, 1939.

Foner, Philip S., ed. *Clara Zetkin: Selected Writings*. Chicago: Haymarket Books, 2015.

Jones, Mike, and Ben Lewis, *Clara Zetkin: Letters and Writings*. London: Merlin Press, 2015.

Marxists Internet Archive: www.marxists.org/archive/zetkin/index.htm.

Puschnerat, Tânia. *Clara Zetkin: Bürgerlichkeit und Marxismus*. Essen: Klartext Verlag, 2003.

Riddell, John, ed. *Founding the Communist International: Proceedings and Documents of the First Congress, March 1919*. New York: Pathfinder Press, 1987.

————. *The German Revolution and the Debate on Soviet Power*. New York: Pathfinder Press, 1986.

————. *Lenin's Struggle for a Revolutionary International 1907–1916*. New York: Pathfinder Press, 1984.

————. *To See the Dawn: Baku, 1920—First Congress of the Peoples of the East.* New York: Pathfinder Press, 1993.

————. *To the Masses: Proceedings of the Third Congress of the Communist International, 1921.* Historical Materialism Book Series, Chicago: Haymarket Books, 2016.

————. *Toward the United Front: Proceedings of the Fourth Congress of the Communist International, 1922.* Historical Materialism Book Series, Chicago: Haymarket Books, 2012.

————. *Workers of the World and Oppressed Peoples, Unite! Proceedings and Documents of the Second Congress, 1920*, 2 volumes. New York: Pathfinder Press, 1991.

Taber, Mike, ed. *The Communist Movement at a Crossroads: Plenums of the Communist International Executive Committee, 1922–1923.* Historical Materialism Book Series, Leiden: Brill, 2017.

Trotsky, Leon. *The Struggle Against Fascism in Germany.* New York: Pathfinder Press, 1971.

————. *The Third International After Lenin.* New York: Pathfinder Press, 1996.

NOTES

1. Bordiga's report can be found in Riddell, ed., *Toward the United Front: Proceedings of the Fourth Congress of the Communist International, 1922* (Historical Materialism Book Series, Chicago: Haymarket Books, 2012), 402–23.
2. Dimitrov's report can be found in *VII Congress of the Communist International: Abridged Stenographic Report of Proceedings* (Moscow: Foreign Languages Publishing House, 1939), 126–29. It can also be accessed at Marxists Internet Archive.
3. *The Communist,* no. 6, June 1936, 489.
4. Trotsky's basic writings on the rise of Nazism in Germany can be found in *The Struggle Against Fascism in Germany* (New York: Pathfinder Press, 1971). Much of this material is also accessible online at Marxists Internet Archive.
5. The four published volumes containing Comintern congress proceedings and edited by John Riddell are *Founding the Communist International: Proceedings and Documents of the First Congress, March 1919* (New York: Pathfinder Press, 1987); *Workers of the World and Oppressed Peoples, Unite! Proceedings of the Second Congress, 1920* (New York: Pathfinder Press, 1991); *To the Masses: Proceedings of the Third Congress of the Communist International, 1921* (Historical Materialism Book Series, Chicago: Haymarket Books, 2016); and *Toward the United Front.* The three supplementary

volumes are *Lenin's Struggle for a Revolutionary International 1907–1916* (New York: Pathfinder Press, 1984); *The German Revolution and the Debate on Soviet Power* (New York: Pathfinder Press, 1986); and *To See the Dawn: Baku, 1920—First Congress of the Peoples of the East* (New York: Pathfinder Press, 1993).

The Struggle Against Fascism

1. Miklós Horthy was the leader of the counterrevolutionary regime in Hungary following the overthrow of the Hungarian soviet government that had existed from March to August 1919.

2. Otto Bauer was the leader and theoretician of the Austrian Social Democratic Party. He was part of the centrist Two-and-a-Half International that had merged with the right-wing Second International at a congress in Hamburg on May 21–25, 1923.

3. Georgia, formerly part of the tsarist empire, became independent following the October 1917 Russian Revolution, with a government led by the Menshevik Party that was hostile to Soviet Russia. On February 16, 1921, Red Army troops entered Georgia in support of a local rebellion by pro-soviet forces. Georgia soon became an independent Soviet republic linked by treaty with Russia.

   A portion of Armenia, formerly divided between the Ottoman and Russian empires, became independent after the First World War, under the rule of the Dashnaks, a nationalist party. In September 1920 Turkish forces attacked the country; in November, as Armenian military resistance collapsed, Soviet troops entered the country in support of a rebellion by pro-Soviet forces, leading to the creation of the Armenian Soviet Socialist Republic.

4. For the September 1920 Italian factory occupations, see the introduction.

5. A reference to the fascists' "March on Rome" of October 22–29, 1922, at the conclusion of which Mussolini was asked to form a cabinet.

6. On July 31, 1922, the Alleanza del Lavoro—grouping the CGL federation and other unions—declared a general strike against the Mussolini regime, to begin the following day. Coming after waves of fascist attacks carried out with virtual impunity and amid growing working-class demoralization, the poorly organized strike met with a weak response by workers, as well as fierce repression. As a result, the leaders capitulated and called off the strike on August 3.

7. A reference to the Ninth Congress of the International Women's Suffrage Alliance, which met in Rome May 12–19, 1923.

8. Wilhelm Groener was Germany's railway minister, who had taken actions to suppress a nationwide strike of rail workers in February 1922.

9. The Italian Nationalist Association joined Mussolini's Fascist Party in March 1923.

10. A reference to the Christian-democratic Italian People's Party.

11. A reference to the fascist unions, called corporations, which were supposedly "common organizations" of labor and capital.

12. The Versailles peace treaty signed June 28, 1919, between Allied powers and Germany, included among its provisions, the transfer of 10 percent of Germany's territory to France, Belgium, Denmark, and Poland, and called for Germany to pay $33 billion ($461 billion in 2016 dollars) in reparations to the Entente powers.

13. Hugo Stinnes was one of the most prominent members of Germany's capitalist class, with a vast, multifaceted economic empire.

14. On January 11, 1923, 60,000 French and Belgian troops invaded and occupied the Ruhr region of Germany—the center of its steel and coal production—in an attempt to exact war reparations following Germany's failure to pay them under the terms of the Versailles Treaty. The occupation lasted into 1925.

15. Literally "trampled cheese spreads out but does not grow strong." From Goethe's *West-östlicher Divan*. The lines that follow clarify Goethe's meaning: "Hammer it firmly into a strong mold and it takes on form—a strong brick for construction."

16. A reference to the *Proletarische Hundertschaften* (sometimes translated as "proletarian hundreds"), which were workers' militias for self-defense against the threat of rightist paramilitary attacks and assassinations. They were first organized on the initiative of the factory-council movement in Central Germany in February 1923. The German Communist Party sought to build these into a national united-front movement that could also be utilized in the fight for revolutionary power. By May 1923 tens of thousands of workers were enrolled in their ranks.

Resolution on Fascism

1. International Red Aid, established by the Comintern in late 1922, defended class-war prisoners worldwide. Clara Zetkin served from 1925 as its president.

Appendix A

1. The term "dictatorship of the proletariat" signifies the democratic rule of working people imposing their will against the violent resistance of the exploiting class.

Appendix B

1. *Protokoll Fünfter Kongress der Kommunistischen Internationale* (Hamburg: Carl Hoym Nachf., 1924), 66–67.

2. From late 1922 on, Lenin had initiated a broad fight within the Soviet leadership around a number of issues, including the national question, defense of the monopoly of foreign trade, and, the alliance with the peasantry. At the root of many of these questions was the growing bureaucratization of the Communist Party, whose general secretary was Stalin. To wage this fight, Lenin had formed a bloc with Trotsky, urging him to champion their common positions on these questions within the party leadership, and he had called for Stalin to be removed as general secretary.

3. For Trotsky's view of these controversies, see Leon Trotsky, *The Third International After Lenin* (New York: Pathfinder Press, 1996), part 2, section 4, 107–15.

4. In his report to the June 1923 ECCI meeting, Zinoviev admitted, "At the time, to be sure, I did have reservations" about the united-front policy. In Mike Taber, ed., *The Communist International at a Crossroads: Plenums of the Communist International Executive Committee, 1922–1923* (Historical Materialism Book Series, Leiden: Brill, 2017).

5. *Protokoll Fünfter Kongress der Kommunistischen Internationale*, 335–39. For the record of the Fourth Congress, see *Toward the United Front, Proceedings of the Fourth Congress of the Communist International*.

6. Tânia Puschnerat, *Clara Zetkin: Bürgerlichkeit und Marxismus* (Essen: Klartext, 2003), 296.

7. For the text of Zetkin's letter, see www.marxists.org/deutsch /archiv/zetkin/1927/10/zkkpd.html.

8. Puschnerat, 305–6.

9. Gilbert Badia, *Clara Zetkin, féministe sans frontières* (Paris: Les

Éditions ouvrières, 1993), 276–78.

10. Ibid., 278. For the text of Zetkin's letter, see *Beiträge zur Geschichte der Arbeiterbewegung*, 6 (1991), 787–88.

11. Zetkin's 3,500-word text was published in *Internationale Presse-Korrespondenz*, vol. 8, no. 64, 1172–73 and no. 65, 1189–90. For a quite different criticism of the draft program, see Leon Trotsky, *The Third International After Lenin*.

12. Puschnerat, 364–66. The entire proceedings of this ECCI meeting are found in Tânia Ünlüdag, "Die Tragödie einer Kämpferin für die Arbeiterbewegung," *IWK* 33 (1997), 337–47. For the controversy involving Kun and Zetkin in 1921, see *To the Masses: Proceedings of the Third Congress of the Communist International*.

13. Puschnerat, 370.

14. Ibid., 370–72, 377, 380.

15. The "theory of the offensive" was advanced by majority leaders in the KPD following the adventurist "March Action" of 1921 to justify their policies in launching that action and to propose that such policies continue. The theory called on Communists to radicalize their slogans and initiate minority actions that could sweep the hesitant workers into action.

16. Zetkin's record of her discussions with Lenin on the Third Congress is included in *To the Masses,* 1137–48. The entire text of Zetkin's *Reminiscences of Lenin* can be found on the Marxists Internet Archive site.

17. Puschnerat, 381.

18. Ibid., 378.

19. One exception has been noted. In 1932 Zetkin assented to her editor's insertion into a message of greetings she had written of a reference to Stalin as an "outstanding and brilliant leader." See Puschnerat, 384.

20. Badia, 288–89, Puschnerat, 374.

21. Puschnerat, 376.

22. Zetkin had defended Luxemburg at the March 1926 ECCI

plenum against similar attacks made in the German party. Her speech was published in the record of the plenum.

23. Puschnerat, 377; Badia, 282, 290.

24. Badia, 300–301.

25. Ibid., 264.

26. Ibid., 302–3.

27. Translated from www.marxists.org/deutsch/archiv/zetkin/1932/08 /alterspraes.html. For the entire text of Zetkin's Reichstag speech, see Mike Jones and Ben Lewis, ed., *Clara Zetkin: Letters and Writings* (London: Merlin Press, 2015), 169–73, or Philip S. Foner, ed., *Clara Zetkin: Selected Writings* (Chicago: Haymarket Books, 2015), 170–75.

INDEX

ABOUT HAYMARKET BOOKS

Haymarket Books is a radical, independent, nonprofit book publisher based in Chicago.

Our mission is to publish books that contribute to struggles for social and economic justice. We strive to make our books a vibrant and organic part of social movements and the education and development of a critical, engaged, international left.

We take inspiration and courage from our namesakes, the Haymarket martyrs, who gave their lives fighting for a better world. Their 1886 struggle for the eight-hour day—which gave us May Day, the international workers' holiday—reminds workers around the world that ordinary people can organize and struggle for their own liberation. These struggles continue today across the globe—struggles against oppression, exploitation, poverty, and war.

Since our founding in 2001, Haymarket Books has published more than five hundred titles. Radically independent, we seek to drive a wedge into the risk-averse world of corporate book publishing. Our authors include Noam Chomsky, Arundhati Roy, Rebecca Solnit, Angela Davis, Howard Zinn, Amy Goodman, Wallace Shawn, Mike Davis, Winona LaDuke, Ilan Pappé, Richard Wolff, Dave Zirin, Keeanga-Yamahtta Taylor, Nick Turse, Dahr Jamail, David Barsamian, Elizabeth Laird, Amira Hass, Mark Steel, Avi Lewis, Naomi Klein, and Neil Davidson. We are also the trade publishers of the acclaimed Historical Materialism Book Series and of Dispatch Books.

ALSO AVAILABLE FROM HAYMARKET BOOKS

Europe in Revolt: Mapping the New European Left
    Edited by Catarina Príncipe and Bhaskar Sunkara

The German Revolution, 1917-1923
    Pierre Broué

The History of Italian Marxism: From its Origins to the Great War
    by Paolo Favilli

The Lost Revolution: Germany 1918 to 1923
    Chris Harman

The Nazis, Capitalism and the Working Class
    Donny Gluckstein

To the Masses: Proceedings of the Third Congress
of the Communist International, 1921
    Edited and introduced by John Riddell

Toward the United Front: Proceedings of the Fourth Congress
of the Communist International, 1922
    Edited and introduced by John Riddell

ABOUT THE EDITORS

Mike Taber is a longtime socialist activist and editor. He has edited or prepared dozens of books on the history of the revolutionary and working-class movement, including books by Leon Trotsky, V. I. Lenin, Malcolm X, James P. Cannon, Che Guevara, and Maurice Bishop.

John Riddell has been a socialist activist and editor since 1960. He has written many books documenting the history of the working-class movement. Riddell also taken part for many years in trade unions and anti-war, solidarity, and climate justice movements.